God was he

God was here first

Ann Hubbard

GOD WAS HERE FIRST

First Edition, 2019

Printed in the United Kingdom
Copyright © 2019Ann Hubbard
No part of this book may be reproduced or transmitted in any form or by any means, electronic, mechanical, photocopying and recording or by any information storage and retrieval system without written permission from the author.

Ann Hubbard, Esthers For the Nations
www.esthersforthenations.org.uk

All scripture quotations, unless otherwise indicated, are taken from the Holy Bible: King James Version.

Cover Design by: Phoebe Stone
Edited by: Sade Fadipe
Published by SERVANT BOOKS www.servantministries.co.uk

This book is a memoir. It reflects the author's present recollections of experiences over time. Some names and characteristics have been changed, some events have been compressed, and some dialogue has been recreated.

The advice and strategies found within may not be suitable for every situation. This work is sold with the understanding that neither the author nor the publisher are held responsible for the results accrued from the advice in this book.

God was here first

MY DEDICATIONS

❖ To God my Heavenly Father, to Jesus Christ my friend and to the Holy Spirit, who helps me, in so many ways.

❖ To John my husband and best friend; I thank you for your patience, encouragement and for always being there for me. I could not have done this journey without you.

❖ To my wonderful children, Richard and Alistair - you are both such a blessing.

❖ To my beautiful granddaughter, Leah, thank you for your help.

My Dedications

ACKNOWLEDGEMENTS

Michelle Hedger my oldest friend, we have laughed and cried together through the years. When I needed to talk and let off steam, your listening ear and caring support, was always near: especially during Alistair's several episodes in hospital. How can I thank you enough!

Joyce Stacey and *Jean Letch* for being such godly neighbours. Without you both being available to help in an emergency, this story may not have been the same and that includes my spiritual journey. I thank you for being close by.

Eastgate European School of Supernatural Life, thank you for the two years of spiritual impartation and guidance resulting in radically changing me as I evolved into all that God meant me to.

Dr Antoinette Phiri, Pastor of The Oasis of Love Ministries International, Zambia, thank you for your friendship. The prophetic word you gave, propelled me to write this book.

Peter Carter our Senior Leader at Eastgate, your prayers for me before I went to Zambia changed me forever!

Esthers, your prayers have sustained and helped me get to the goal post. God fulfilled his word to me in saying, "You will have many

Acknowledgements

children." I had no idea my children would be scattered around the world.

Florence Sutherland, President of Esthers for the Nations. Thank you for being my prayer partner and friend. As your Vice, I have not been as available as expected but you have been gracious towards me and never moan at the extra work this has caused.

To all *Counselling Clients* that have cheered me on to write this book. I hope you continue to find strength in Christ.

Contents

MY DEDICATIONS	v
ACKNOWLEDGEMENTS	vii
INTRODUCTION	11
Chapter 1	15
HUSH!	15
CHAPTER 2	37
MAGIC AND WITCHCRAFT	37
CHAPTER 3	51
MISCARRIAGES, BIRTHS, DOCTORS, AND HOSPITALS	51
CHAPTER 4	81
DOES HEALING STILL HAPPEN?	81
CHAPTER 5	97
HEAVENLY EXPERIENCES	97
CHAPTER 6	121
DO I NEED DELIVERANCE?	121
CHAPTER 7	133
TAKE AUTHORITY!	133
CHAPTER 8	155
AN OPEN DOOR FOR *'Annabel'*	155
CHAPTER 9	171
ANGELS	171
Chapter 10	209
THE POWER OF THANKFULNESS	209
CHAPTER 11	231
GOD MAKES OUR PATHS SMOOTH	231

Contents

CHAPTER 12 265
END FOR NOW 265

INTRODUCTION

The blows and fiery darts of life can be hard to bear and if anyone had told me, I'd one day share my life with the world; I would have discarded the idea as ridiculous. I had been introduced to a life of secrecy from the age of three and certain aspects of my life were to be buried under the carpet never to be spoken of or heard about – never to be exposed. The enemy's plan for Ann Hubbard was that she be tucked away from public view, possibly wallowing in sorrow: bordering on insanity.

However, I was about thirty years old, when I felt the Holy Spirit say, "Keep a journal of your life." Although I kept one for a short while, like most New Year resolutions, the habit soon faded away. So, twenty years later the Holy Spirit brought back the idea of writing a book. I asked what the book would be about, and He made it clear; the book would be about my life and it would help many people.

While attending a Pastors' Wives Conference in Zambia with Apostle Florence Sutherland as the Guest Speaker, I was again reminded about writing this book. My role was to support the conference with counselling and ministry needs, as required. Unknowing to me, God had other ideas. After listening to an inspirational message by Apostle Florence, I had an immense

Introduction

desire for an anointing to teach the Word of God and to see The Word change people's lives. I prayed for opportunities to speak to crowds of people and to share the great things God had done in my life, and how His Word had helped me. I felt uneasy about my prayer requests as I mostly held a supportive ministry - away from public glare. I soon realised it was the Holy Spirit urging me to pray.

No one would have guessed that the conference's main speaker would fall ill and be unable to lead the conference the next day. I was busy preparing to play my role as scheduled, when our host, Pastor Antoinette phoned to confirm (as a doctor) that Apostle Florence was too ill to minister; she had prayed before calling and believed God wanted me to share His word.

I turned to the Holy Spirit, shocked and confused but as I prayed about this turn of events, I felt God's calm reassurance. I also sensed that He wanted me to teach on having no other gods besides Him. He led me to the scriptures warning about the dangers of witchcraft and idols - wanting me to use examples from my own life and the journey He had taken me through, permitting me to share about my time in heaven.

That was how I found myself ministering during both the morning and even the afternoon sessions, under God's anointing. I yielded myself as God's vessel and he ministered powerfully through me.

Both my translator and host Pastor joined in with the audience to experience God's presence and anointing at the end. Some people wept in repentance and some received His love in a greater measure than ever before. The ministration exceeded the scheduled time and God was glorified.

At the end of the conference, whilst we were in the pastor's lounge, Pastor Antoinette turned and pointed to me saying, "You must write a book. It will help many people." It was as though God was speaking through her. Suddenly, I lost control and doubled over as the power of God hit me like a shot of electricity.

After ministering in Zambia, I returned home and resumed to the second year of studies at (my church's) European School of Ministry. I had missed the first two weeks of term and they were now on a module called, "Destined for Destiny" which was releasing us to dream and geared our thoughts into action. I felt I had already experienced the topic in an even more practical way, whilst in Zambia and now overjoyed by the theoretical teachings of how to put my dreams about the book into action. Again, I considered this as another confirmation that God wanted me to write this book.

This chronological recount of my life from childhood to adulthood unfolds from innocence, influence, causes, consequences, trauma, love, and Grace. It reveals the impact of negative influences and

Introduction

how the enemy seeks to destroy our destinies without us even knowing.

Most of all it reveals an all-seeing ever-knowing, loving God who desires to fellowship with His creation.

At the heart of this Book and during the trials and traumas of life I faced, God was very present, lifting me, loving me and talking to me through it all.

Is it possible that God took me through these trials just for you?

He wants you to know that no matter what you may be going through; whatever the abuse you may have suffered; the loss you may have experienced; the marriage breakdown or break-up lurking, the *Balm of Gilead* is yours and He will never leave you nor forsake you.

God was here first

Chapter 1

HUSH!

HUSH!

I sweat profusely, as we climb the hill to the children's fairground. My brother Gavin's six-year-old legs make bigger strides than mine. At three years old, I am super-excited as Gavin holds my hand tightly; aware of his promise to take care of his younger sister. His friends call out to him in their thick Irish accents, but I have spied the swing-boats, so I drag my brother towards the rides.

We watch them for a while, as I jump up and down with excitement. I plead with my brother for us to have a turn on them. He agrees. But as my brother steps on to join me, this big, older man whom my brother knows pushes him aside and gets onto the ride with me, instead.

I am scared and as the swing-boat soars higher than I thought it would. Clutching onto the rope, I see the big man smiling at me – but not like the smiles I am used to, and this makes me shift in my seat. I wish my brother was here. He beckons me over, "No!" I shout, but he insists. Lonely and unsure, I stumble towards him, glad it's only a short distance. When I look up, I notice he is undoing the buckle of his belt then he lifts me onto his lap. Uncomfortable in this position, I try shifting but he unzips his trousers. At three years old, I know that boys should have nothing to do with my underwear, so I protest as he proceeds to molest me.

To stop me from screaming, he covers my open mouth with his big clammy hand. I can't breathe, so I bite down as hard as I can - he gasps in pain and scorns, "Plucky youngster!" while lifting me off his lap.

What a relief! I gasp for fresh air and wobble back to my seat, feeling odd. The ride is slower now and soon comes to a sudden halt. I sit frozen, with my excitement about the ride destroyed. I hear the operator ask, "Are you all right?" My brother looks at my face and asks the same thing. I start to open my mouth but stop when I see the man with clammy hands, now bent over me. He whispers 'If you tell anyone, your brothers will lose their jobs. It's our secret'."

I remember feeling frightened as I looked up at him and thought, "I don't like you! Aren't you the man who pays my brothers 6d for working at your pickling-onion factory for a few hours on a Saturday?"

From then on, I became fearful and out of fear, I told no one. To everyone else nothing had happened, although my mum said I went from being an angel to being, a little devil as I would wake up during the nights screaming, due to repeated nightmares.

That was the first of many secrets not told and not remembered for many years.

On the home front, we had a maid who was fixated with reading frightening stories. I still liked her as she would take my sibling and I out in our pushchair, to exciting places.

She would puff with great effort, from pushing our double pushchair up the steep hill to her mum's house. I loved her mum; she told us about her life as a gipsy - dancing around campfires and eating rabbits. I didn't like that bit though, because I had a pet rabbit. As they danced, someone would play the fiddle or mouth organ. We spent many happy hours in her back garden, playing in her gipsy caravan and imagining the horses taking us from place to place. Each time we finished a cup of tea, she would look inside the cup mysteriously, tip out the tea leaves and tell us what it foretold. When I tried doing this, I saw nothing. She would then play the piano and I would watch with fascination as the metronome swung backwards and forwards, making a clicking rhythm, in sync with the beat as she played.

On the way home, our maid would make sure she had our attention and reminded us, "You mustn't tell your mum where you have been. If you do, she will stop us going back there and you enjoy hearing all my mums' stories, don't you?" I also kept this a secret from our mother.

Many years later, I found out that our mother (on agreeing to take our maid on) had expressly forbidden that we mingle with our maid's family as she knew her mother to be of a wild character. I don't know what happened to our maid, but she disappeared from our lives suddenly. She also disappeared from my mind as I had other things to think about.

CHASE THE DOG

My family was waiting outside our house, in the car, and ready to go to the seaside. My sister and I were sitting in the back with our puppy whom we named Chase when my brother realised he had left his beach ball behind. I remember my dad instructing us to hold onto the puppy. As my brother opened the car door before we could restrain the dog, he leapt out of the car! Suddenly we heard screeching brakes and a crunch! I was stunned. The driver apologised but said he couldn't have avoided him. Mum kept saying to Dad, "That could have been one of us."

Somehow, we knew our puppy was dead when Dad and the driver picked him up and disappeared with him. We wanted to follow them, but they did not allow us. We later learnt they had buried him in our garden after a fox dug his body up and left it on top of the dirt. In those days, they didn't believe in exposing children to death. I don't remember if we went to the seaside that day, but I do remember crying. We all missed Chase. My parents tried replacing Chase with kittens, but our chickens chased them, and the kittens kept disappearing.

Hush!!

We now lived in Ireland differed from Scotland: where we had lived previously. My earliest memory was being asked if I was Protestant or Catholic by other children. Whether they would be my friends or not rested on my answer. We went to a small private preschool above a chemist shop, where sweets were sold. My memories of the school are good, apart from learning to write by joining dots. It was so boring, I thought, "Surely, there is a better method than this." However, the hot chocolate and stories around the open fire made up for any flaws the school had. When I left preschool and started at the same school my brothers attended, I was in shock. Finding myself in a class of over 30 children, with no hot chocolate, no stories around the open fire and no rest after lunch, was strange. I felt out of place as everyone dashed to get to their classrooms. I remember tales my brothers told, of desks being thrown out of windows and chairs were thrown off the roof.

To my humiliation, I suffered regular nose bleeds which were difficult to stop. One resulted in me being admitted into hospital - my first experience of being left alone.

As a child, I was prone to having accidents - one nearly ended up blinding me. I was watching Dad cut wood for our new bunk beds when I accidentally stood on a plank of wood with a nail in it. It rose and hit me just above my eye. Dad rushed me to the hospital while Mum held a cloth over my bleeding face, "An inch lower and you would have lost your sight," the doctor had said. Luckily, I was left with just stitches and a scar.

Soon after this, my baby sister had a narrow escape with meningitis. I remember visiting her in hospital and only being allowed to wave at her through a glass screen. After they released her from isolation, we moved to England.

A NEW HOME IN ENGLAND

The boat trip from Ireland to England, in 1955, was exciting until we hit a storm and were confined to our bunks. Everyone on the boat, apart from my family, became seasick. Eventually, we arrived in London. I vividly remember our arrival as being noisy. There were so many cars and people seemed to be in a hurry.

Crossing the road to Hamleys Toy Shop was terrifying! Mum and Dad held our hands tightly, but I soon forgot my fears as we watched the demonstration of Moving Toys. My brothers brought a remote-control car each, and us girls brought dolls. We stayed the night in London and drove to our new house the next day. It turned out to be a very large four-bedroom bungalow. I remember running from room to room. It delighted my brothers to find that the previous owner had left a cage full of pet mice and a swivel office chair. We made ourselves dizzy, taking turns to be swirled around. My parents were not too pleased but had other things on their minds. The furniture had not arrived and in fact, didn't turn up for another week. It should have been on the same boat as ours, but it had missed the sailing. My sisters and I went back to stay at the hotel in London, which suited my dad as he worked nearby. My brothers went to stay with an aunt who lived in London.

Our new home called *The Spinney* had acres of land, an orchard which adjoined open fields and a river. We attended the local Catholic school, but life there was cruel. They teased us because of our accent, and the teaching method was very different, so we all struggled. I was forever being told off for not listening. The teacher would rap my knuckles or throw the blackboard rubber at me and if it did not hit me, it hit my best friend Susan who sat beside me. We both gained many a bruise, but my brothers fared worse. Once, I painfully watched my brothers wince, as the teacher brought the cane down as hard as he could - about six times!

One of my worse memories is being told off after struggling to read in front of my class. My punishment for not being able to read was to stand in the corner wearing a large dunce's hat, which my classmates found quite funny. I have no recall, of how long I stood there for, but it seemed a very long time. Worse was to come as they gave me a nickname, which stuck with me, especially out in the playground. From then on, I hated school and for many years after, I found it hard to read out loud. I never fully recovered.

I was soon admitted into a hospital because I would often wake up at night screaming with earaches. After my mum had given me a hot water bottle, she would ignore my screams, explaining that she had to get some sleep. I felt very lonely being in pain. After a routine hearing test, it was discovered that I was profoundly deaf and had been lip reading for probably, about two years. The audiologist had a student in the room who noticed I was lip reading. The doctors couldn't identify what was wrong me and had a practice of hanging up X-rays, seeking specialist opinions. Once, a visiting consultant noticed something on the x-ray which the others had missed. When the doctors operated on me, the visiting-consultant was proven right - they found infected cotton wool inside my ear canal which resulted in the ear infections and blocked sinuses. After a week in hospital draining my sinuses, I was prescribed antibiotics and allowed home, but had to be off school for nearly a month. As I left the hospital for the first time, I heard birds sing, and people seemed to shout when talking. I returned to school and my classmates were pleased to see me. I soon made more friends.

The time we spent at *The Spinney, in Sutton Coldfield, Birmingham* went by quickly. Some memories are of me getting stuck while climbing a tree after copying my brother, who had to rescue me. We had amazing picnics in our garden; we would run off and play on a swing, hanging from a tree branch. One day, I went higher than usual but hadn't considered the height, so I jumped and ended up in the rose bushes. That was painful!

Learning to horse-ride at the stable directly opposite our bungalow was also a memorable experience. My sister mounted on a smaller pony called Shandy, but they allocated me a much taller horse named Tom. Tom and I were doing well until he went from trotting to galloping, and the next minute it felt like we were flying. I remember the teacher shouting, "Pull back on the reins!" I didn't know what she meant; it was my second time ever, on a horse! But Tom had other ideas, and we were racing towards a gate, leading onto a road. The teacher was pacing behind, frantically trying to catch up with us and shouting, "Pull back on the reins!" I was having trouble holding on, let alone pulling back on the reins! With the gate looming in front of me, I finally pulled back on the reins with all my might. The suddenness of Tom stopping not only took me by surprise; I went flying right over Tom's head and hit the ground with a thud! I was okay, though slightly shaken. No way was I getting back on that horse again! I had told myself. My teacher insisted and with much apprehension, I climbed back on. She encouraged me to speak to Tom, who by then had calmed down. After many months of learning to ride at the stables, our trainer said we were now proficient enough to be allowed to ride on the road. We were excited and looking forward to doing this until our parents informed us that we would be moving to Brighton.

So, there we were, on the move again, and I was heartbroken about leaving my new best friend Susan at school. As a leaving gift, she gave me a picture of a ballet dancer in Swan Lake which made me cry for months every time I looked at it. Although being near the seaside was exciting, I found it strange living in a rented house surrounded by the owner's possessions. They had left a doll's house as tall as me in my bedroom, (complete with miniature people and furniture) which I played with for hours. We soon discovered the arcades and dodgem rides in Brighton. We were thrilled to find out that local children, including us, could ride for free, during the winter period.

My first experience of my new school in Rottingdean was abusive and very confusing for me. They forbade me to write with my left hand and would tie it behind my back, which hurt. When my mum heard about this, she was furious! I felt sorry that she had to deal with all five of us on her own as Dad still worked in London, and only came home at the weekends. Mum told us, after speaking with the headmaster, that he saw nothing wrong with forcing me to write with my right hand. My mum withdrew all her daughters from that school and enrolled us at another private school.

Feeling a little lost at this new school, we stood out as the only children not wearing school uniforms. The three of us clung together during break times. I remember the other children staring at us. In making friends with them, I soon found the courage to ask them why they stared. It turned out they had never seen three sisters before. This was strange to us, being used to large families in Ireland.

The teaching methods were, once again, different. The school gave no consideration to us about this. Maths and English seemed like a foreign language at first, and I was forever being told off for having the last word. I didn't realise this until a teacher took me aside and said, "Ann you are a bright child and polite, but you do have a bad habit of wanting to have the last word and teachers believe you are answering back."

Looking back, I thank God for her honesty, as I changed from that day onwards and finished my days there a much happier child. My teacher's belief in me changed my perspective on how I saw myself. Plus, I was allowed to write with my left hand - what a bonus!

Soon after we moved to Brighton, I started a babysitting job and would daydream as I walked over the Downs in Brighton to babysit a Spanish baby whose parents soon introduced me to fortune-tellers. I was hooked and fascinated by how the craft worked and would spend my income from babysitting on visiting fortune-tellers every Saturday. However, I got disillusioned as they all had something different to say about my future. Until I met this fortune-teller who reminded me of our maid's gipsy mother back in Ireland. She took my hand and read my palm; telling me about my life so accurately it frightened me. I don't remember what she said, but from then on, I felt as if I was being followed, so I stopped seeking fortune tellers.

BROGRAVE GARDENS & THE ORPHANAGE

When I was nine years old, we moved into a new house in Brograve Gardens, Beckenham, Kent. Much to my relief the feelings of being followed stopped once we moved to Beckenham. With some anticipation and slight fear, I was to start my sixth school at Beckenham Covenant which was also a private school. I was fearful of having to negotiate the different teaching methods. This was both a day and boarding school. I didn't fit in and was very unhappy there as I was incessantly bullied. Once, I remember saying to myself, 'Sticks and stones don't break your bones and words can never hurt you.' I was walking home that day with other kids trailing behind, calling me names. Thinking back on this still hurts because words do hurt, and that saying is nonsense!

In my loneliness, I turned to books. Not having a television also added to my problems after my dad removed it because we did not do our homework. We were disoriented and shocked when the television first disappeared. However, on the plus side, not having a television had its advantages as it drew us together as a family and we turned to playing board games. I started a new hobby of stamp and postcard collecting. One negative side to no longer having a television was not being able to join in at school with conversations about favourite television programmes like *Top of the Pops*, and I felt left out.

My respite was at the weekends. I passed time at a Catholic orphanage, where I helped look after the toddlers and eventually graduated to the babies. I remember entering the room and seeing a sea of babies sitting on the floor and others in cots. I soon became adept at changing babies on my lap; I did one after another. Although I was not to interact with the children, I did. I used to make the babies laugh, but this was frowned on by the other nursery nurses as it slowed down my work.

Every afternoon, nursery nurses would put all the babies in their prams (often two into the same pram) and take them out to the garden for their daily dose of fresh air. The nursery nurses would leave me in charge and disappear behind the shed for a cigarette. Rarely did a child cry; maybe because they knew no one would come. When a child disappeared, I would wonder what had happened to them. One day I asked, and I was told that a family had chosen the child - this was a good thing, they had said.

It was sad for me as I missed them. Then, there was one little girl I had become quite fond of and when I asked why she was still there, they informed me, in whispers, that she had never been out of her pram before she came to them. I could not imagine this, as I remembered the times we had enjoyed playing with my baby sister on the floor. They also mentioned another reason, was the possibility of her being schizophrenic like her birth-mother. I did not understand what this meant, but it sounded bad and I tried to get my parents to adopt her but without success.

The staffs always welcomed me and were glad for another pair of hands. They loved having me join them for dinner as I listened, enthralled by their stories. Telling me how poorly paid they were and threatening to leave and become nannies did nothing to put me off wanting to become one of them. Their lives sounded like the perfect life for me and I imagined myself, becoming a nanny or nursery nurse in the future.

MIDNIGHT GUESTS

One night I looked around and discovered myself in a different location to my bedroom. Knowing I had gone to bed as normal, I was curious to know where I was and what was happening. I noticed people standing next to me. So, I asked who they were, and where I was. One of them replied, "You are in training to be a witch and we are your guardians and will watch over you." It did not feel real and at first, I enjoyed watching them perform their tricks. They loved to show off; I remember saying to them "Where are your broomsticks?" They laughed and said, "We don't need them, but we will fly on one if you like." and they produced one. This went on for many nights. I would suddenly find myself back there with them. I later found out they were using astral projection.

I enjoyed observing but never got involved in doing any of their spells and tricks. Thinking no one had noticed, one day at school I heard a voice say, "Blow up the laboratory." At first, I thought I had misheard, but then realised it was one of the 'guardians' so I refused. The same night they brought me in front of their witches' council, who threatened to beat me up if I didn't do what they instructed me to do. Bravely I replied, "You can't do that because my parents will know." The one in charge retorted back, "We have ways of doing it, without leaving a mark on your body." I became frightened and said, "I want to leave!"

After the discussion with the council, they decided to allow me to leave as I was still a child but threatened to hurt members of my family if I told anyone.

Shortly after this, my sister broke her leg in a freak- accident and I took it as a warning. Years later, when I remember this, I ask, "Did I dream this, or did it happen?"

Life went on and the bullying stopped after a serious accident. We were camping in Italy by a beautiful lake. I was about to sit down to eat when I misjudged the height of the camping stool. So, I grabbed the camping table to stop myself from falling off the stool but causing the table to tip. The table of contents including a freshly made, steaming pot of tea poured over my bottom half. My dad reacted quickly by sweeping me into his arms and ran to put me under running cold water. Minutes later, I knew we were heading for the hospital. My sister Pat was in the back of the car with me, where I squatted as I could no longer sit down properly. I felt as if I was in a fog, on hearing my dad desperately trying to get people to understand (his English) that he needed directions to the Hospital.

At the hospital, the doctors gave me medicine to take the pain away, as my swimming costume was being taken off. I didn't understand what they were saying as they spoke Italian. Then one must have spoken English, as I heard him say I had third-degree burns at the top of my legs and I would have to stay in hospital for two to three months. During this time, I learnt to speak a little Italian, understanding more than I could speak. The extraordinary coincidence was that my dad had taken out an accident insurance policy for the first time which covered the private hospital fees.

I was admitted into hospital, during the holiday season so my siblings were thrilled, by the extra holiday time I needed to recover. But one night when they didn't come to see me and my new friend (in the next bed) discharged, I felt abandoned and wondered why my family had not come to the hospital. The next day, when they visited, my mum was not her usual, cheerful self. The previous night during the heavy downpour, our tent flooded; soaking all our possessions. The only dry clothes they had were the ones they were wearing. My mum decided she had enough of camping, so they all went to stay in a local hotel, much to my dad's dismay.

Now it was the end of the season, and the hotels were closing. Also, my dad couldn't take any more time off work; having already taken over a month extra. My hospital consultant told my parents I had to transfer straight away to a hospital in England as they could not release me without fully recovering. All I remember of the journey to catch the ferry is feeling itchy and being told I mustn't touch my burns even though they itched dreadfully. Dad had to drive slowly as every bump was painful, but it concerned him that we would miss the boat. After a phone call, the ticketing agency somehow persuaded the operators to hold up the ferry for us, knowing there would be an ambulance waiting at the other end.

When we eventually arrived at the ferry passengers lined the rails wondering who was so important to hold up the boat. The sailors carried me on a stretcher, up the stairs and onto a cabin bed; I remember the people staring and me feeling embarrassed. My brothers could not resist waving as if they were the queen. My parents were passed a message by the captain of the ferry, informing them that because of the delay, the ambulance waiting for me in England could not wait any longer and the hospital had agreed to my going home for the night - much to the relief of my parents. When the Burns Specialist at Guys Hospital examined me the next day, they couldn't believe that a third-degree burn accident had not needed skin grafts. They kept asking what the doctors in Italy had done, causing them and me great frustration as I couldn't answer their questions. They decided I was healing so well that I could go home but was told to stay in bed for another couple of months. They instructed that on no account should I burst any blisters. A nurse came in to change the dressings each day, which I found painful, but she used to make me laugh by telling jokes as she dressed my burns.

One difference I found out later was that the Italian doctors believed in fresh air; not lots of dressings. My dad's quick reactions of cooling my burns down by rinsing the tea leaves off probably helped too. I had to have a metal contraption over the top of my legs to keep the bedclothes from touching the burns, and to allow air to aid the healing. I also used the contraption as my table.

At first, it was fun missing school but after reading every book in sight, I couldn't wait to go back. I could not even receive visitors because of the risk of infection. My brothers and sisters could only stand in the doorway of my room. All I remember is how difficult it was, resisting the urge to itch as the burns healed. I knew if I did, I would cause myself even more pain.

When I returned to school, I was treated like a celebrity! The school had been praying for me. The bullying stopped, and I did well in school but having missed so much school work I was continually behind.

GCEs Vs BABYSITTING THE MILLIONAIRE KIDS

I decided not to do my GCE's because a millionaire couple that I used to babysit for, asked me to look after their two children, aged seven and nine, whilst they stayed with their grandparents at a spa hotel in Switzerland, for a month. It sounded more appealing than staying at school doing GCEs.

Little did I know that the little girl would not sleep on her own! I had to go to bed at the same time, she did. Also, their grandparents didn't want us to leave the hotel as this was too much for them.

They allowed us to swim in the pool attached to the hotel, but the children were adventurous and protested at this. After a row with the grandparents, who were not budging, I rang their parents who told them I was in charge.

It was a strange experience. The grandparents accepted their two grandchildren but treated me as hired help even though I wasn't getting paid. I made friends with the staff and most were students. It shocked me when I got shown their living accommodation It was appalling, bearing in mind they worked in a hotel frequented by millionaires; you had to have money to have stayed there.

I befriended a nanny looking after eight children, most of whom had different dads: the result of four divorces. She had me in stitches with stories of the different dads and their requirements. Birthday parties were a nightmare, as each of the dads would try to outdo each other and she had to remember whose aunt was whose. We would meet up when we could but chatting with her made me realise I didn't want to be a nanny anymore. I also didn't enjoy being treated like a hired-help.

God had not dealt with my pride by then.

Hush!!

CHAPTER 2

MAGIC AND WITCHCRAFT

By the time I returned to England from Switzerland, I had changed so much that I found my school friends quite childish. We now had little in common, so I turned to books. Unfortunately, I came across books by Author Dennis Wheatley and found myself becoming fascinated with reading about the occult. I read through Wheatley's Black Magic series. It was, however, the last chapter in the series that completely changed my life! Dennis Wheatley had a strange writing style. One minute he was writing fiction, by the next, he had attracted the reader into the occult world, using activation diagrams - he even slotted in some prayers. Not understanding the reality or implications ahead, I carried out the instructions within the chapter and ended up sacrificing my life to Satan.

That same night, after reading through the final chapter, I experienced an incident never to be forgotten. To this day, I don't know if it happened, but I do remember it all too vividly...

I went to bed as normal and awoke, only to find myself standing in what appeared as a temple surrounded by people in black cloaks with hoods over their faces. Two of the hooded people grabbed me and tried to dress me in a white garment. As they did, I noticed a baby's body on the altar, with blood dripping from it. Some other hooded people quickly removed the body, which made me realise they intended to put me on the altar, instead. I screamed in protest and tried to get away, but they tightened their grip around my arms and it hurt. They said, "It will help you if you drink this." Others held my head and forced me to drink something bitter, and I felt myself relax.

I must have fallen asleep, as I remember waking up, paralysed with fear and unable to move. Hovering above me, was a man wearing a goat's head mask. I tried to scream but could barely make a sound. Then I heard chants (from a distance) to the words, "The bride of Satan"

When I awoke, I found myself on my bedroom floor, with my bedclothes wrapped around me. I was relieved at the thought of it being just a nightmare, but I was so disturbed by what had happened, that I never read another one of Dennis Wheatly books, or any other books about the occult and got rid of all the ones I had. I wanted no reminder of what happened, though nothing I had read could be compared to what I had experienced that night.

BILLY GRAHAM - SAYING YES TO JESUS

Two days later, I met someone at the bus stop who appeared to know me. I later discovered she was a neighbour of ours called Glynis. She invited me to a Billy Graham Conference in London the next day. Going to London appealed to me and I was surprised when my mum agreed if only my sister accompanied me.

Magic & Witchcraft

Going on a train was a new experience as everywhere I looked, was surrounded by people. Glynis turned out to be in the class above me, at my last school. I had been so caught up with wanting to go to London that I had not enquired what the conference was about and even when she said, "Jesus" I was none the wiser. Glynis was a helper at the conference, so not only did we sit in superb seats near the front, we did not have to queue to get in!

There must have been over a thousand people, sitting in the theatre. The singing was beautiful, and people expressed their joy by dancing within the aisles. The songs were so different from the hymns sung at my Catholic Church. That day, Billy Graham's message stunned me as he spoke about a loving, Heavenly Father, who sent his son Jesus to die for me.

He emphasised that I now had forgiveness for all my sins. In all my years as a Catholic, the priest had never mentioned a loving father, instead, he hammered in about a God who would punish me for my sins. Billy Graham had said that this loving Father wanted a relationship with me. When he made the altar call, I responded by standing and prayed the salvation prayer with hundreds of others. Then, he gave an invitation to those who had stood up for the prayer, "If you were serious about asking Jesus into your lives, make your way to the altar and I will pray for you." I tried to get my sister to go along with me, but she showed no interest. I joined the others; impatient to get to the altar. Whatever was on the inside of me did not like my decision and shouted, "You don't want to do this!" So, I tried returning to my seat, but to no avail, for I was surrounded by people all heading in one direction – the altar. When I got to the front, I noticed people crying while some fell over as Billy Graham prayed for them, and this frightened me. Soon it was my turn to be prayed for. To my surprise, an electric wave surged through my entire body as he put his hand on my head. The experience left me with an unexplainable inner peace. Then we followed a lady into a room, set aside for those who had asked Jesus into their lives. They were all given a small book to read but somehow, they missed me out and I ended up not getting the small book. When my friend Glynis, asked a few days later if I felt any different, I looked at her as if she were mad and wondered why she had asked such a ridiculous question; was I meant to feel any different?!

Soon after the conference, I started dating boys. Both my brothers insisted on chaperoning me, on my first date with a friend of theirs. Walking behind me, I convinced them I would be alright. Although their matchmaking didn't last long, I dated my next boyfriend for several months.

During this time, my oldest brother gave me a twenty-pound note, saying, "Ann, you are pretty, but you wear dark, old-fashioned clothes! Boys like to see girls in bright colours." I needed no second bidding and soon bought myself some new, bright-coloured clothes. Up until then, I had thought I was fat and ugly. I was often teased and called 'fatty'. Luckily, my eldest brother's words were not only soothing, but they dissolved my fears about being fat and ugly.

I soon noticed, that ever since the Billy Graham Meeting, things had started going well for me. I prayed about my GCE English language exam, (which I took at a secretarial college) and I felt a sense of peace. I found the examination paper quite easy and finished with more than enough time to recheck what I had written.

With good English grades when the result came out, I had no problem getting a job. It also helped that my brother's girlfriend's dad was a director at Unilever where I applied for a job. I still had to pass a stiff entrance exam, in which I got one of the highest marks they had ever seen. I was offered a job there and then as a secretary - starting in the typing pool. The training was thorough as they demanded a hundred per cent accuracy or else the supervisor returned the work, for retyping. I worked there for three years and was promoted to the dispatching station for faxes. The dispatching station role was so different from being in the typing pool. There were people from all over the world, phoning in with information that needed to be faxed. My job was to touch-type what they dictated over the phone. One minute it was for a television commercial, another, could be part of a formula for a product. Every day was different, and although I was using my typing skills, I was not using my shorthand skills enough, to keep my speed up to standard.

I left Unilever with a glowing reference and over the years, I held various secretarial jobs all over London. Once I landed a cushy job working for a temporary agency as a stand-in, which meant being paid even when I had no work assigned.

One day, they sent me to a high-end advertising agency. As I walked in, the officials all walked out to attend a meeting, leaving me with no instructions on how to contact them, or what to do. All day, I did nothing but answer the phone, blagging it.

I decided soon after this that I'd had enough of travelling to London; standing in crowded train carriages during heat waves and dripping with sweat. I secured a local job straight after, at almost the same rate of pay. This time, it was as secretary to the Parts Manager at K.J. Motors Headquarters - a large garage chain.

I soon met a boy who worked in the parts department and after several years, we were engaged. When we discussed sex, the idea of it seemed exciting. I pushed aside my religious convictions of 'no sex before marriage'. The argument in my head kept insisting it was okay as we planned to get married. To cut a long story short, I ended up getting pregnant.

When I broke the news to my fiancé, his expression of shock and horror told its own story. After talking it through, we both agreed the timing was far from perfect. I knew I could no longer delay the inevitable task of telling my parents, having managed to hide the pregnancy from them for months. With fear and trepidation, I mustered up enough courage to speak to my mum. Her response was "What will the neighbours think? You can't keep the baby here!" My dad said, "I'm disappointed in you!" which hurt to the core.

I felt so ashamed and hurt that they didn't like my boyfriend - they made this quite clear. His parents advised an abortion and introduced us to someone, who was able to point us in the right direction. We agreed it was the best option, as I had convinced myself it was not the right time. I had to attend a Marie Curie clinic where, after questioning me, they agreed with my decision. I was booked into a private clinic at the cost of £200. My dad insisted that the boyfriend paid half, and he covered the rest of the bill.

Now over four months pregnant, I awoke on the day of the abortion scared at the prospect. No one explained this was a real baby. It was simply referred to as a foetus. In those days, there were no scans. I made the mistake of asking how they were going to do it as they anaesthetised me. The doctor explained they would use 'suction' to suck the baby out. I shuddered and almost changed my mind. Then I remembered my parents would not allow me to stay at home and that my finance didn't want the baby either. Afterwards, I was told it was a girl.

While recovering at home, I developed a high temperature, so my mum called the doctor. Instead of the doctor judging me, she was tender, caring and compassionate. When she said, "I need to tell you this womb infection might affect your ability to have any more children." the seriousness and guilt of what I had done hit me, and I started to cry. The thought that I could have been the mother of a baby girl, and now being told I won't have any children, was devastating. The rest of my family did not know what had happened.

This was another secret kept under wraps.

I was still sore from the abortion when I heard my finance had made another girl pregnant! I felt sick. At first, I thought he could never have been unfaithful. Then I started having doubts. I remembered various instances. One was when he had taken me to meet a girl in her home with her little boy. While there, I thought she was being over-familiar with my boyfriend but before I could approach him about it, his best friend confirmed my worst fears. 'My boyfriend' had taken me to meet the very girl he had impregnated alongside me! My best friend Susan advised me not to return the engagement ring he bought me, as he planned to give it to the girl. What a scoundrel he turned out to be! My parents were relieved when we split up, but I was heartbroken and felt betrayed.

Needing a change, I switched off completely from dating boys and decided I needed a fresh start. So, I applied for and secured a job in New York. I was due to start it in four months' time, which gave me ample time to sort out a work permit. I also planned to move out of my parent's home and find a flat to share with my friend Glynis. To help cover the rent, we would advertise for two other girls to join us.

A SMILE THAT CHANGED MY LIFE

John almost ran me over at work, as he raced around a blind corner in a customer's car! He stopped, apologised and gave me a beaming smile, at which my stomach did a flip. I would never have guessed that a smile from a boy at work could change my life! The boy asked me for a date, a few days later and I responded with a firm "No, I'm going to New York." He came back with, "I'm going to Australia." So, I decided to go out with him, both agreeing to a temporary affair.

John was easy to talk to, and by the second date, we sat in the car talking for hours. Once, my dad startled us when he knocked on the window, reminding me he had to lock the back door. We continued seeing each other most days enjoying the time spent together.

Several months later, he invited me to his house with a hidden agenda to meet his parents. I kept reminding myself of his planned move to Australia and awaited his sailing dates to be confirmed. I knew his friend had changed his mind about migrating, but John already had a job waiting for him.

As we walked into his house, he picked up an envelope marked 'Australia House'. He put it down and we tried to carry on talking, but the letter's presence felt like an elephant in the room.

I said, "I don't mind you opening it." My heart was in my mouth, as he slit open the envelope. He looked at me and said, "It's my sailing date in a couple of weeks!"

My heart sank. He must have read my mind.

"I'm not going." I heard him say.

I could not believe what I had heard, I breathed a sigh of relief! Unknown to him, I had also decided not to take the position in New York. Before I could process what John had said, his parents walked in on us, surprised to see me. His petite mum had a strong

Scottish accent and beamed the same beautiful smile as her son. In no time, a large plate of sandwiches arrived. I had no trouble understanding her as my dad was Scottish and I was born in Scotland, which did help. We all laughed and got on well with each other. His mum kept saying, "You must be special. He's not brought anyone home before!"

SECRETS TO TELL, OR NOT TO TELL

I still remember the day, months later, when John asked me to marry him. He seemed vague, distracted and quiet, as we drove towards his house. In my mind, I thought something was wrong. Is he breaking up with me?

He turned, and to my surprise asked, "Will you marry me?" and immediately went back to focussing on the road. I was so taken aback. I didn't answer at first, even though I wanted to throw my arms around him.

Later, John told me that my hesitation was shouting, *'No!'* He continued, "I can't cater for you to the standard you're used to. I live in a council house, I'm a mechanic and your dad could object to us getting married." He wasn't aware that I loved him even more for his concern about what my dad might think.

Then came the day when he had to approach my dad about his intentions towards me. Walking up to our house in Manor Way reminded him of our first date. He had almost chickened out, after seeing where we lived. Though this time, he said the house appeared larger and more intimidating than ever before. Again, he summoned the courage to knock on the door, reminding himself he could do this.

It took a while for John to ask my dad for his permission, but he eventually did, while next to the manure heap within our garden. My dad expressed his concerns about us not having enough money to live on, and John being able to keep up with the standard of living I was accustomed to. John replied, "I will not always be a mechanic, I intend to work hard and become service manager." This statement must have reassured my dad, and he gave us his blessing.

Unaware up until then that others considered us wealthy, John's parents voiced the same concerns as my dad. By this time, my brothers and sisters were clamouring to hear the news. They welcomed John into the family with a glass of champagne and talked about dates when we should get married. We agreed to wait until we had saved enough money for a deposit on a house.

Then I faced the dilemma of my past and thought: "We can't get married with secrets!" I was plagued with dreams of John leaving me once I told him about the abortion. I would wake up in a sweat, crying. So, I rehearsed what I would say and how to approach it in my head, again and again. Each time, I would end up crying. One day, as planned in my head, I asked for us to go for a drive to our favourite place: a peaceful, calm place. When he had switched off the engine, I blurted out - not how I planned it, "What I am going to tell you might change your mind about marrying me." I steeled myself, convinced he would be disappointed and ashamed of me, let alone want to marry me.

John looked me in the face and said, "Nothing will make that happen."

After listening to my outburst, he lifted my head saying, "Before you, I went out with several girls. I am sorry about the abortion and all you went through. I never liked or trusted your previous boyfriend. All this happened in the past. We are now living in the present."

Sat in shock, I had to ask: "So, you still love me and want to get married?" At which he grabbed and kissed me. We got married one beautiful Autumn day in September of 1972.

My plan before meeting John had been to start afresh in New York, but God obviously had other plans for me.

CHAPTER 3

MISCARRIAGES, BIRTHS, DOCTORS, AND HOSPITALS

Miscarriages, Births, Doctors, And Hospitals

We didn't go away on a honeymoon as we could not afford one. We had just bought a terraced house, having both worked like crazy to gather enough money for the deposit. We were content with the little money we had and didn't care. After our second year of marriage, we started trying for a baby, much without success. I had several early miscarriages, and then nothing. My doctor referred us to a fertility clinic after which sex became a duty, not pleasure as it was now scheduled and restricted to the time of the month and my temperature. I was certainly sure, that not conceiving was God's punishment for having an abortion. Then came the day at the fertility clinic, when we were told there was something wrong between us. It was explained that the chances of me ever getting pregnant were slim. On the next visit, much to the doctor's amazement, I tested positive.

I kept the news to myself and did not tell my work colleagues, which turned out to be a big mistake.

At this time, I had a fantastic local job and was able to pop home at dinner time to prepare our evening meal. I worked in a local architect's office as a Personal Assistant to the CEO, who employed many architects and young trainees. One day, they played a trick on me and burst a balloon behind my back. They almost scared the life out of me - I was so startled, I dropped the papers I was holding and suddenly felt cramps in my stomach. I dashed to the toilet, where I realised my worse fear. I was bleeding. I told my boss about my condition; he was very compassionate and sent me home.

I did not lose the baby but had to stay in bed for the first three months, as I kept spotting. This fully convinced me it was God's punishment for the abortion. John's mum came to look after me and we grew close. In her eyes, I could do no wrong. I would pray to God that nothing would happen to the baby even though guilt and condemnation plagued my thoughts. The hospital monitored me closely and in due course, I gave birth to a beautiful, baby boy on the first day of March in 1976, whom we named Richard. Apart from turning blue when born, Richard was a perfectly healthy child.

Imagine my surprise when nine months later I fell pregnant again! We were so pleased, and apart from being given oestrogen injections and iron tablets, I had a normal delivery in January 1978.

Alistair (whose name means mighty warrior) was impatient to come into the world; he arrived ten weeks earlier than his due date and weighed 3lbs 6ozs. As soon as he was born, he was taken to the intensive care baby unit, without me seeing or holding him. The consultant came back and said he was underweight; his lungs had not quite formed and the next few hours were crucial. From the moment he was born it was touch and go; if he would survive. One week he would do well and the next, be on the danger list; we lived

Miscarriages, Births, Doctors, And Hospitals

in constant suspense of what might happen next. They only allowed us to touch him through the portholes of the incubator. We became friendly with other parents only to go back in to find their baby had died or been discharged. We encouraged each other, but it was a silent unit apart from monitoring machines.

Weeks later, I was so frustrated at not being able to hold my baby. I watched nurses lift him; change him and I thought, "I could do that." I longed to hold him, and my heart ached for this to happen. One day, during ward-rounds, I asked the consultant if I could hold my son. I felt I could care for him, having watched the nurses several times. His reply was unpleasant as he angrily questioned if I valued my baby's life and siting that I was a danger to my own child.

I burst into tears and something on the inside of me died. The bus journey home seemed to take forever as I held back the tears. I remember looking and reading the congratulation cards, almost to remind myself we had a baby, and he was ours. Back at home, I continued to pack boxes in preparation for the planned 'house move'. I could not stop myself from thinking if our new baby would ever be with us. Tears fell as it hit me; he might not live, and I would never get to hold him. The thought of going to see Alistair the next day was too much to face, which relieved John in a way, as he would come home from work, wash, and we would be out the door. Up until then, I had visited the hospital every day for at least two hours and some evenings, whilst the neighbours had Richard.

One nurse noticed that we hadn't been for two days and on the second day phoned and asked if everything was okay. I told her what the consultant had said; she said, "if you can come over now, I will allow you to hold your baby." I rushed around, convinced a neighbour to give me a lift, another one had Richard and I arrived at the hospital, so excited. I noticed as she handed Alistair to me, she wore a big silver cross around her neck. She said, "This could cost me my job if anyone finds out." Then she put Alistair in my arms. He was so small; wrapped in a baby blanket at first it worried me - I might harm him. She encouraged me to hold him close, being careful not to pull on any of the tubes and monitoring discs attached to him.

As I held Alistair, she monitored him closely and got excited when his body temperature rose, which until then, he'd had trouble maintaining. He was so small in my arms being not much longer than a safety pin and weighing about 3lbs as he had lost weight. I gazed in wonder as I finally embraced the little fighter. I felt like a mother again; for up until then, he seemed to belong to everyone else.

Alistair did so well out of his incubator. They also allowed John to hold him for the first time that night. He started to gain weight and a short while later; he graduated out of the incubator into an open incubator and was pronounced 'out of danger'. We were allowed to hold him whenever we wanted to but most days, I sat by his crib praying for our little fighter.

Now weighing 5lbs, he was doing so well, and they allowed him to come home at five weeks old - when he still should not have been born.

GOD CAN DO IT

I sat staring at the door, willing someone to come out. Why are hospitals such lonely, empty places? Wasn't it just fifteen minutes since the sister had come out of that same door and said, "You'd better phone your husband!" The dread those words evoked, increased my heart thumps as the wall clock flashed with lights and doctors rushed into the room Alistair was in. Oh, John, hurry! I need you. I knew it would take over an hour for him to get to the hospital from his work.

It had not surprised him when I phoned to say Alistair was in the hospital. My mind raced through all that had happened in the past few months. Last week, we had been so happy. Finally, bringing Alistair home from the Special Care Baby Unit at Medway Hospital; remembering that against all odds, he had survived. His brother Richard, now eighteen months, was so fond of his little brother.

I had expected problems, but nothing could have prepared us for the three-hourly feeds that took an hour and a half to give. It was such a slow process. We knew this would take time as he was used to being fed by a tube. Somehow, we expected all the problems to go, once we had our baby home. After six days of this, we were both exhausted. The night before, Alistair seemed restless, shifting around in his crib; he did not wind. I had changed him; cuddled him, tried everything. In desperation, I woke John up and told him Ali was not taking his bottle. John also tried winding him. Again, nothing. We were both concerned as he seemed listless and pale. We talked about calling the doctor but decided he would not appreciate being called out at 4 am. Neither of us could sleep. I sat cuddling Ali, willing him to take his bottle. Eventually, he took a little and I breathed a sigh of relief. John, Ali and I slept fitfully.

The morning seemed like a long time coming. I tried Alistair on his bottle again. This time he choked as he gulped down a little milk. I changed him and noticed he seemed cold and listless. I put him in front of the fire and phoned the health visitor. It seemed ages before she picked her phone up. I tried not to panic and reassured myself, she'll know what to do.

I got through; her response was one of urgency. "Take him to the doctors." I needed no second bidding. I grabbed Richard, who was still in his pyjamas, dumped him on the carrycot (with his brother in it) and ran down the road, to my best friend, thinking about how glad I was that she lived close by. My best friend didn't know what had hit her! I apologised, as I left her Richard, who was still in his pyjamas and yet to have his breakfast. "He can wear Adams clothes. Go!" she cried.

The doctor's receptionist said I will have to wait. I felt frustrated as she did not seem to understand the urgency. Sat outside the doctor's door was a queue of four people ahead of me. Looking at Alistair, they sensed he needed urgent attention. As tears welled-up in sheer frustration, one of the ladies asked me what the matter was. By then, Alistair was pale and motionless. While thinking of what to say, the buzzer went and the lady next in the queue turned and said, "You go in." I beamed at her and walked into the doctor's room, apprehensive. His face confirmed my fears. "Not her again!" he seemed to say. I had been to the doctors several times in the previous week. First for a cold, then with Alistair being sick. As I spoke, he took one look at Ali, snatched him from me and got his stereoscope to listen to his heart. I wondered what was happening and watched on, as he prepared an injection. I noticed his hands trembling. All within a flash, he had the phone under his chin, instructing the receptionist to order an emergency ambulance.

He had just finished giving Ali the injection when the ambulance men arrived. They had to wait for him to write the notes. He told me that Ali had been in a state of collapse. The injection's dosage was that of an adult's and he had just a few seconds to work out the dosage for a premature baby as too much would have been dangerous; too little would have been too late. I sat in the ambulance, cuddling Ali and feeling reassured as he was now a lovely colour; as if nothing was wrong with him.

The doctor seemed annoyed when we arrived at the hospital. "What's all the fuss about? He only has double pneumonia." She asked me to agree to a routine lumbar puncture. I wondered why they left him with no clothes on and longed to pick him up and cuddle him. Double pneumonia. That sounded serious.

At last, John was holding my hand. His presence and touch were comforting. His response calmed me down as I poured out my fears when the nurse came out of Alistair's room, looking like she had been crying. Flashing lights and doctors with equipment materialised from nowhere, heading into Ali's room. Double Pneumonia… Voicing my fears helped.

The Ward Sister appeared relieved to see someone who could tell us what exactly was happening. "The Consultant would like a word with you." I stared at her face, trying to read it but got nothing. I tried questioning her. "The consultant will answer your questions." She ushered us into this freezing room with one chair and insisted I drank a cup of tea with loads of sugar, which made me gag. The consultant came in, apologised for the room's temperature, but by then I was shivering and thinking, "This cannot get any worse, or can it?"

I will never forget his words, for as long as I live… "There is no easy way to tell parents about the bad news. Your son has immense brain damage and will be a vegetable." I looked at John, who was looking at me. I wanted to ask questions but was struck dumb with shock. I felt as if my heart was breaking, and life had stopped. I was aware of what was going on, but I felt removed, at the same time. This is someone else's baby they are talking about, surely! I came back, as he said, "We are trying to get him into a London hospital, but we do not think he would survive the journey."

We both asked at the same time, "What had happened?"

"During the routine lumbar puncture, his heart stopped. We had three teams working on him as we also discovered milk on his lungs when we did the lumbar puncture. We tried resuscitation and had almost given up when he breathed on his own accord. The time he stopped breathing was way over the limit."

We went home, silent in the car and still in shock.

It helped to know Richard was having fun with my friend's sons. I could also speak to her about Alistair. She kept saying Alistair came into this world for a reason; it will be alright. She offered to have Richard for as long as necessary.

I went upstairs and collapsed in tears. My heart hurt. I looked around but there was no crib. Where was it? John had put it on top of the wardrobe which distressed me even more. I fell on my knees. "Please God, do not let him die. Please don't let him die. I will do anything but don't let him die. It does not matter if anything is wrong with him. Just let his heart be strong and let him live. I will sacrifice him to you." Recalling bible teaching of Sampson in the temple, I had heard at church but somehow, this felt wrong. Then I heard an audible voice say, "I want you!" Instantly, I knew what this meant. "I will dedicate my life to you but please let him live." Afterwards, I had an overwhelming sense of peace and knew Ali would live. I ran down the stairs to tell my husband. "Alistair is going to live!" He turned, looked at me calmly and said, "Yes, I know."

Just then, the phone rang it was the hospital informing us there was a Catholic priest on his way to baptise Ali. On getting there, we were ushered into a side room, large enough but full of equipment surrounding his cot and a large oxygen canister behind him. I was distressed to see his little face covered by an oxygen mask. There were wire discs all over his tiny body and machines beeping every second. He lay there, so still.

The priest's voice went on. My husband nudged me. "Yes, his name is Alistair Sydney Hubbard." This is not happening... I was recalling Richards christening - such a happy occasion. Suddenly, I realised no one in our families were aware Alistair was back in hospital, let alone the seriousness of it. Tears rolled down my face. He is a fighter, this is all wrong! I kept telling myself (almost wanting to stop it and toying with telling the priest to stop and go!) Alistair is going to live!

At last, it was over, and we could go home. There was no response from Ali as we said goodbye. Both John and I were too frightened to touch him, in case we set off the machines.

Back home, we sat in silence, willing for the phone to ring to say they had got Ali into a London hospital. Great Ormond Street had agreed to accept him, we were told. A doctor and two nurses would go with him in the ambulance and they would inform us when he arrived. When we said, "We would follow the ambulance" they advised us not to, as they had a police escort and they would be speeding.

TO TRANSFUSE OR REFUSE?

The minutes seemed to drag by endlessly once we knew they had started the journey to Great Ormond Street. Would they have arrived at Great Ormond yet?

As soon as Alistair's ambulance set out, we drove to Bromley, where John's mum lived. When we phoned to find out if our son had reached the hospital, to our frustration, the line was engaged. We tried again, but it rang, and rang, till finally, we heard, "Great Ormond Street. How can I help you?" The joy of speaking to someone who could help us was immense. Once we explained who we were, the receptionist put us through to Doctor Matthews, (Alistair's consultant) in Room 5a of the Intensive Care Unit. He introduced himself and tried to reassure us that Alistair's condition seemed to have stabilised though he had been put on oxygen. Later, (he explained) they would try a mixture of Ali breathing for himself and oxygen. I sighed with great relief; the consultant seemed so positive.

By this time, we were phoning the hospital from my mother-in-law's house. As soon as we put her in the picture, she insisted on looking after Richard and advised us not to delay being with Alistair; we needed no second bidding and set out. After driving around in circles, we finally found the correct entrance to Great Ormond Street Hospital for Children. Luckily, we saw a parking space and parked in it, feeling relieved, only to see a parking attendant staring at us. I said a silent prayer; praying he would understand our situation. "Was that your baby with the police escort?" he asked. Which till today still astonishes me, as I know ambulances come and go all the time. So how did this parking attendant know about our baby? I wondered. It was such a relief to hear him say, "I will allow you to park this once but you're in the doctors' and consultants' car park." We did not realise the tremendous favour that had occurred until afterwards. We found out later that parking attendants do not allow anyone to park where we had under any circumstances and we never saw the parking attendant again.

We stood outside Room 5a and I remember being put off as we could not just enter the room. We had to press the bell and were asked to wait outside as someone would come along to talk to us. As the minutes ticked by, we grew apprehensive. After what seemed like a long while, the consultant came out, ushered us into a small room with a bed in it, and this time, two chairs. He introduced himself with a lovely, welcoming smile. He explained his position as the consultant in charge of the unit and Alistair's case. My first impression when speaking to this kind, sincere and caring man over the phone earlier on was confirmed.

He told us to go over every little detail, from Alistair's birth to the present; asking us questions and prompting our memory on important facts. We waited patiently for him to update us on Alistair. "Since our phone conversation, I am afraid Alistair's condition has deteriorated, causing him to have several monitors and equipment. One of the equipment entailed having a mask over his face to help him breathe called a ventilator. Another tube goes down his nose to his lungs, to help suck out fluid from his lungs." He carried on, "Sometimes, this can be upsetting for parents and I would like to prepare you ahead." By then, I had built a picture of tubes coming in and out of him, from every part of his delicate body.

The reality, when I finally set my eyes on Alistair, did not live up to the awfulness my imagination had created. Although not being prepared would have been traumatising. My baby lay motionless, surrounded by equipment: two enormous, oxygen canisters beside his cot. We hardly recognised him; a big plaster covered his face, holding in place the ventilation mask and tube. His body and head were covered in discs, monitoring different reactions. His arms had syringes connected to drips. Machines beeped, others made different noises, while the drips flashed. One, I recognised, monitored his heart and breathing. Not knowing what any of the readings meant, I watched the lines fluctuate, finding it strangely hypnotic. Two nurses were stationed to him, observing his condition. I recall my detachment as I looked on and asked myself if this was happening to me.

At this stage, we both could not take it anymore. Alistair's room was hot, stuffy and noisy. We decided to take turns going out for a breather whilst the other person stayed. All this time, the consultant watched us like a hawk - I suppose, summing us up. He decided that we could take it, and quietly informed us that Alistair was critically ill, and he would like us to stay nearby.

Rochester, where we lived, they believed was too far. John's mum lived in Bromley which they considered near enough. So, they offered to pay for a hotel for us which we declined, wanting to get back to Richard and some sense of normality. Our world had turned upside down. Would it ever go back to normal again?

We moved to Bromley and John's mum willingly took over caring for Richard. She not only looked after Richard but took care of us, when there. She aimed to give us nothing else to worry about other than going to see Ali. Everybody was marvellous. John's work gave him unlimited time off. They even provided a car and filled it up with petrol. Our neighbours in Rochester looked after our house. The support we got took all other worries off our shoulders.

We soon became used to the equipment and the machines around our son, but I never got used to that horrible feeling when an alarm went off. Sometimes it meant the drips needed changing, but other times the alarm alerted them he had stopped breathing and needed a gentle probe and he would start breathing again. I never lost the thought, that it could one day be the end, though my heart kept telling me he would be alright. Nonetheless, what we witnessed said precisely the opposite.

These visits to the hospital went on for several weeks, by which time John had gone back to work. Alistair's condition had now become critical. They had done an E.E.G, which monitored his brain and showed unusual brain patterns. I later found out this was an electroencephalogram. He started having fits; his little body would jump up in the air, then thud back down on the mattress. This would happen about ten times within a short period and I couldn't help thinking he would injure himself. My heart sank every time I witnessed this; I felt so helpless. As a last resort, they asked for our permission to use steroids, explaining the long-term effects, one was being infertile. We agreed, and I prayed Alistair would not hold our decision against us.

After using the steroid, the fitting stopped and the fluid on his brain was reducing; he seemed to have improved. Thankfully, he was moved from the critical list and although he was placed on the danger list, we were relieved, not to witness him fitting anymore. During this time, two nurses were with him day and night, sucking out the fluid on his lungs every half an hour and tenderly giving him a mouthwash now and then.

We ran out of what to say to him as we had been encouraged to talk to him rather than chatting with nurses. People who had been unconscious remember hearing people's voices in conversations. Some-times music helped. We tried self-consciously singing to him. We even relayed all his brother's latest antics to him. Often, the nurses would try not to laugh. John and I used to have great discussions on whether he held onto our fingers tighter than last time.

Did his eyes just flicker? I was looking for anything positive; still believing he would be okay. Even though all the signs said otherwise. Discs now covered most of his little body and the nurses had to shave his lovely blonde curls off to insert even more tubes and lines. The nurses' tears dripped on his head whilst doing this.

I remember once meeting with the consultant who again asked us to describe all that had happened, this time from conception, yet again looking for clues. This time he was crying with us, while turning over all the pages of tests done, in trying to find out what had caused pneumonia. He explained this is always a secondary infection and they needed to find out the primary cause.

Alistair was once again back on the critical list with the general opinion being, no hope of change. He told us there was a strong possibility of Alistair having long-term damage to his nervous system. He explained that they had tried every option of treatment available. Then determination rose from within me and I said, "Mind you, he is a fighter." Not knowing Alistair's name meant fighter. The tense atmosphere seemed to lift, and everyone's attitude changed. The consultant looked at me, said, "Yes, I believe you." It seemed, from that moment on, the consultant and his team became even more determined that Ali would live. Still, no matter what they did, he remained critically ill.

Acclimatising to the stifling heat in the new, smaller room Alistair had been moved into proved difficult for John and I. Now, only one nurse was constantly with him. The smallness of the room made John claustrophobic. While the uncomfortable, suffocating heat often caused him to dash out to the coolness of the corridor's ward, taking a short break and returning bravely.

Every day was different at the hospital; I had met other mothers who also stayed in the parent's accommodation. We supported each other, laughing and making up outrageous stories to give ourselves a form of relief. Whenever I mentioned Alistair was in the 5a intensive care unit, silence followed as they knew it was the ward for critically ill children. When I went to visit a baby in the heart unit, I thanked God I didn't have to live with an infant waiting for a heart transplant or with heart defects. These mothers were honest with me and said they felt the same about Alistair.

Travelling home each weekend by train, I cherished the normality and fresh air. I enjoyed the moment as I was able to focus on Richard and John rather than Ali. Richard would not let me out of his sight when I got home and cried when I left. My heart pulled in two directions. It was now over a month since Ali's admission; going from critical to dangerously ill and back again.

Miscarriages, Births, Doctors, And Hospitals

We decided that John's mum needed a break, so we went back to our house. Now staying with Alistair just three days a week took some pressure off me. Alistair was too ill to have visitors other than us while Richard enjoyed having me to himself. My friends welcomed me back, and some day's life appeared normal. Reality hit when Dr Mathews needed permission from us for further tests.

I noticed how pale he seemed since I last saw him, and guilt overwhelmed me. The doctors expressed concern about the goodness of his blood. This did not surprise me as I sometimes joked that they were vampires. The doctors told us a blood transfusion would be the answer but assured us of their understanding if, for religious beliefs, we did not want this. I explained I was a Christian, and his face relaxed - he smiled a knowing smile. I expressed my fears about who the blood came from: might he catch aids from contaminated blood? I also wondered if the blood would change Alistair's character and personality? They told me that all the blood went through a process of screening out possibilities of infection. This answered some of my concerns.

I signed the permission and they went ahead with the transfusion; telling me they would inform me when I could return in about an hour. I tried to eat my lunch, which tasted like cardboard. Then I decided to walk to the local park where I paced around twice, thinking, "Would they have finished yet?" One hour turned to two.

I prayed and tried not to think of what was going on. They had explained the risks involved in doing this transfusion. When I eventually saw Alistair, my whole body relaxed. The difference was immediately noticeable! His cheeks were rosy, and his body had colour; life seemed to have come back to him. The first transfusion was not successful, so he ended up having two.

THE HARDEST DECISION OF OUR LIVES

Before Alistair's birth, we had looked for a bigger house with a larger garden. We fell in love with the first house we had seen in Cuxton. Now, we were having second thoughts about moving, a decision needing to be made quickly as we were due to exchange contracts. We decided we needed advice from Alistair's consultant. We explained the dilemma to him as we could not afford to move and bury Alistair. He thought it would be a good idea to move, have a fresh start, and they would pay for Alistair's burial. I was glad over the next few weeks to have something to do, by then we were back in our own house. Packing and clearing out took my mind off Alistair until we visited him in the evenings.

The fateful day arrived; we knew it was coming. You are still not prepared to hear the words no parent wants to hear. The consultant said, "I would like to arrange a meeting to discuss the possibility of turning off the life-support machine." At those words, my heart raced. "A team would represent their point of view and we could have whoever we wanted." We sat until late each night at home, discussing all the possibilities with neither of us able to decide. Over the next week, Alistair fought for his life as his heart stopped five times one night. The cardiac team joked about moving into his room and yet another machine added but still, he fought. The hospital had not mentioned turning off the life support again as he was fighting so hard for his life. We realised they could not put it off much longer.

Soon after this, the strangest thing happened. I received a phone call from a nun who said the whole covenant was praying for Alistair. I thought, "How reassuring!" and wondered how they knew.

The mystery was solved when we later found out that an article in the local paper had mentioned Alistair was fighting for his life after being born so premature. Where they obtained the information from we did not have time to find out. God moves in mysterious ways; I kept meeting total strangers who would say the same thing, "We are praying for your son."

We noticed Alistair was now on 90% oxygen and he had gone through two canisters of gas. Once a day, they took blood to test his oxygen levels, using this enormous needle but Alistair did not flinch; I did, at the size of the needle. A second opinion from an eminent visiting-neurologist confirmed Dr Matthew's thoughts that the brain damage was permanent, with a slight possibility of some recovery.

The next day, I expected a phone call saying Alistair had died; I steeled myself for the news. We still had not made up our minds about the dreaded decision. One time we even asked John's mum for her opinion. She turned around, "You are asking me to decide about my grandchild?" It stunned us into silence! It was then, the reality of what we were discussing, hit us. We knew the hospital had made up their minds. As we walked up to the stairs leading to the unit, I remember finding the courage to ask John, "Have you decided?" I was frightened to look at him, and wanted an answer, but not. He stopped, paused, looked at me, and said he thought it was best for Alistair if we switched off the machine. There and then, I realised I agreed with him. There was a sense of relief, having made the decision; no more tossing and turning at night, yet at the same time dreading the loss.

It was a long walk up those final flights of stairs to the unit but when we got to the unit, something seemed different. No one to meet us and tell us what had been happening. We walked into Alistair's room and noticed he was only on 30% oxygen. Nurses were all smiles as we told Alistair all about the move, realising there was a big probability he would be there with us. The nurse or nurses would try their hardest to appear as if they were not there listening, though I caught some of them laughing. By the time

Miscarriages, Births, Doctors, And Hospitals

Richard came to visit his baby brother, they knew him well. The nurses made a big fuss of him and used to take him off to the playroom and play with him. He used to look so funny in a white gown with a mask on. I was glad when they were dispensed of, as we all hated wearing them. This time I did not care if I appeared an idiot as I carried on telling Alistair about Richard's latest antics - falling into one of the moving boxes, which had made me laugh and laugh. The nurse even said she reckoned if he kept with this improvement, he would be out within a few weeks.

Dr Mathews called it a miracle. First on a mixture of oxygen and breathing on his own, to breathing completely on his own. When the consultant proudly placed him in my arms for the first time without an oxygen mask, it seemed very strange. I thought, "Does he know I am his mum?" He nestled into my chest and responded to our voices. It felt so good. What beautiful blue eyes! I did not want to stop cuddling him. Again, the consultant watched Alistair like a hawk, as he breathed on his own and his tolerance with no oxygen support. Alistair surprised everyone, as he continued to breathe on his own with no help.

The next time we visited, they had moved him from 5a to a normal ward attached to 5a. For the first time, he had no equipment on him aside from his feeding tube. They had removed all the discs, and for the first time, he was dressed in a blue baby-grow. I noticed his hair had grown back and was now darker and straight. I realised how comforting the monitors had become and now they had gone, it was so quiet. Dr Matthews told us a few weeks later when we went to take him home, that he had never met a child, like Alistair - such a fighter, and that what had happened to him was the equivalent of a stroke in an adult - it was a miracle he had survived.

We thanked the consultant for saving Alistair's life; "You know, one day you might not thank me for doing so." Slight dread filled me and pondered what he meant. Wanting nothing to spoil this time, I asked about the last tests they had done, one of which was on his eyes. He said there was a slight possibility of some loss of vision, but it was too early to tell yet.

We were so glad to have him home. He could do no wrong in our eyes, but we reaped the results of his being spoilt in the hospital. He would scream for hours, unless you wheeled his pram up and down the room, the motion eventually rocking him to sleep. We were also wary after being told to observe him closely as they still did not know what had caused him to be so ill. One condition of him being allowed home was that he slept in our bedroom, so we could keep a close watch on him.

Richard showed signs of jealousy every time I went to feed Alistair, or when he needed the potty and would find a way of getting my attention. It took a good fifteen minutes to get Ali to feed; he was so slow; it was no joke. I think not having anyone for Richard to play with did not help as we had only just moved into our new house, the day before Alistair came home. My mum came down for a week; scrubbed every cupboard and washed down the walls. She helped me to bring order, and her company brought relief. The next months were very hard, but gradually, I made friends with people who had children of the same age. It also helped that my best friend from Rochester had moved just down the road.

Life seemed to settle into a nice pattern, and Great Ormond Street seemed pleased with Alistair's progress. But feeding became harder. When we fed him, he would go funny afterwards and be sick. I mentioned this casually on one of his monthly check-ups at the hospital. The consultant said he thought he was having epileptic fits and would need to go on a medicine called Epilim. This did not bother us, as we were so relieved that they had found a solution. Over the next few months, his fits got worse. Admitting him for assessment to monitor his fits for a week, they felt, was the best course of action.

In the meantime, I had an appointment with our local hospital, responsible also for Alistair's care. John could not have time off for this appointment. We had decided that it was impractical to keep having time off for appointments: once a month at Great Ormond St and every four months local hospital, plus the possibility of other appointments.

For the first time since our last meeting, I found myself face to face with the paediatrician who had said Ali would become a vegetable. I tried my hardest not to let it show that deep down I blamed the hospital for what happened. It did not help our relationship one bit when he came out with, "You realise your son is spastic and has cerebral palsy and it has affected all of him?" I think the shocked expression on my face must have told him otherwise. The room started to spin. I pulled myself together, thinking, "I need to know what cerebral palsy means."

He said, "You must have noticed that something was wrong. Sometimes it means that they are not great at maths." He must have said much more, but the word 'spastic' was the only thing I remembered. Other than that, I realised by the tone of his voice that Ali would probably never be like other children.

I told him, "We put his condition down to him being so premature and had only been out of the hospital for about four months". I think by then he realised I was in shock.

How I made it home, I will never know. I remember thinking on the bus, "I have a magazine somewhere that has medical conditions in it, maybe that will help." I rushed upstairs frantically looking for the magazine and found the article. I read it again and again, thinking all the time that the consultant was wrong. I told myself there was nothing wrong with his legs or arms but knowing each time I read the facts; Alistair's limbs were stiff. Thinking of how hard it was to dress or undress him. The article stated that these children are incontinent and have trouble walking and talking. It also said there were different types but did not say what they were. It sounded horrible. I sobbed and sobbed until I thought my heart would break. I knew I needed to talk to someone.

I dialled a friend, who came around and kept saying it did not matter. We would all be together at Armageddon; she was a Jehovah's Witness. I kept thinking, but it does matter! He is here now and how am I going to tell John? I asked her, "What has Armageddon got to do with this?" Our friendship cooled after that.

I do not remember John's reaction, but I know his attitude was that it did not change Alistair, while mine was different. I viewed Ali with different eyes and noticed he did not hold a rattle, was unable to roll over and had trouble with feeding. I became empty inside and despondent. After a sleepless night, I phoned Alistair's consultant at Great Ormond Street and told him what had happened. An appointment was made to see us the next day. This time, both of us could be there.

DID GOD JUST SPEAK THROUGH A BOOK?

Whilst waiting, a trolley came along with books that could be purchased. Some were about different health conditions. We bought one on cerebral palsy and it surprised me. I found it hard to believe what I was reading; it did not sound so bad. It said cerebral palsy is when there is damage to the central cortex of the brain. Children with cerebral palsy may be spastic, athetoid, ataxic or floppy and their intelligence may range from normal to subnormal. There may also be handicaps affecting vision, hearing, and speech, specific learning problems and possibly some physical deformity or emotional problems. Many children with lots of help go onto lead a normal life. I hung onto that statement and by the time it came to our turn to see Doctor Matthew, I felt different.

Doctor Matthew was furious with the local hospital and said he was trying to break it to us gently but yes; they were sure Ali had cerebral palsy and he explained what it was. I remember asking him if Ali would walk and he replied that it was too early to say. He held out a lot of hope for Ali. He reassured us, and we left there feeling hopeful that the future was not as black as we had thought.

Reflecting on this, in all the years we were at Great Ormond Street, we never saw this trolley again. The book I bought, had said children with spasticity needed physiotherapy and I remembered the local hospital saying much the same thing. Ali looked so vulnerable as the physiotherapist undressed him but confidently moving his limbs and getting him to laugh. My fears left me. I watched fascinated, as she got Ali to do things I couldn't, and she showed me how to stretch his limbs, called passive movements, and how to lay him down correctly, so he had more movement in his arms. She told me he was quadriplegic which meant it affected all four limbs. She caused me to feel empowered, at last something to do to help him. I asked her if he would be able to walk. Again, I heard, "It is too early to tell, but he was badly affected." I loved doing the physiotherapy and Ali seemed to love it; I looked forward to her coming. It seemed, at last, we could do something to help him. The fact that she said, "He would need extensive physiotherapy at least three hours of doing the passive movements each day," did not alarm me, I felt at last equipped to help him.

CHAPTER 4

DOES HEALING STILL HAPPEN?

I never seemed to have time to talk to my neighbours. I watched them chatting to each other and wishing I could get to know them. They seemed different; I remembered their names were Joyce and Jean, having met them once before we moved in. Another reason I desired to get to know them, as they had children of a similar age to Richard.

It took time, but gradually, I became acquainted with them. In desperation one day, I asked one of them, to have Richard for me whilst I went for a hospital appointment with Ali, in London. They seemed very interested in all the details relating to Alistair; little did I know they were praying for him.

Weeks later, whilst walking back from taking Richard to playschool, Joyce asked ever so casually, If I knew Jesus and if I knew that Jesus healed. She mentioned that the fellowship they both attend prays for people to get healed. This fascinated me as I knew such things had happened in the bible, but not in today's world. Soon after, I asked Joyce and Jean round. We sat in the garden, sipping on coffee. I wanted to know more about this Jesus that healed but every time they started to tell me more about Christ, the kids would squabble, and Ali would cry - it was like all hell, let loose!

In between time, Ali's fits became alarming, and it concerned the hospitals. Great Ormond Street invited him in for drug monitoring and assessment. A few days before Ali admittance was due, the girls finally told me about Jesus. I will never forget the wonder of finding out Jesus died on the cross for me and why he did it. The Bible teaching at school and church suddenly became real. I recalled also what Billy Graham had said. I kept saying I am a Catholic, so I couldn't attend their fellowship. They replied, "We have people from all different faiths."

Ali's stay in the hospital seemed to be routine until late one night, as I approached him to say goodnight, I saw a doctor examining Ali's eyes with a torch. Surprised and alarmed, as the doctor walked away, I tackled him. "Why were you looking into his eyes with a torch?" "Just routine," he had said and carried on walking. I ran after him and replied, "I don't believe you!" By this time, I was alarmed, as I recognised he was evading the truth. I kept persisting until he turned and said angrily, "We believe your son has a brain tumour. We planned to inform you in the morning." I lay in bed, going over in my head, what this might mean and wished I had not persisted for an answer. Now I would have to wait until the morning to find out more. It was a long night…

The next morning, I was informed that they needed to do a magnetic resonance imaging (MRI) scan of his brain, and he would require sedation, to keep him still. This was done by a powerful magnetic field, radio waves and a computer which would produce detailed pictures of his brain whilst he was inside the MRI machine.

Does Healing Still Happen?

These images would show slices of his brain clearer and with more detail than other imaging methods. GOSH was proud to have one of these MRI machines. We were reassured to hear many people had had these scans, safely. The consultant said we could return home for the weekend, but we were to bring Alistair back on Monday, for the MRI.

The possibility of a brain tumour devastated me and all weekend, through every spare moment, I had prayed. Monday came, and Ali was duly sedated. He was so small compared to this enormous machine. They placed his still small body on the conveyor belt and I watched as he disappeared inside the MRI machine. I remember thinking, "I am glad they sedated him, if awake, he would have been terrified." I put on an X-ray shielding-vest, watched the computers as they took images of his brain and I enquired what the pictures meant. I recognised some parts of his brain which did not seem to please them. They turned the screens away from me. What did they not want me to see? I could feel the anxiety in my stomach. Ali stayed another night as he had not woken up fully. It worried me sick, but they reassured me it was just routine.

That night, I stayed awake praying, "Please, God, do not let him have a brain tumour, let him be all right." I kept hearing, "Go and see Joyce and Jean." This carried on all night until I became sick of hearing the same thing. I will never forget, sitting in the parents' sitting room when Alistair's consultant came in. We all gasped, they did not come and get you unless there was an emergency. Apprehensively, I entered his office.

He said, "There is good and bad news, which do you want to hear first?" I opted for the good news. The good news is, there is no sign of a brain tumour. The bad news, I am sorry to tell you, he has severe damage to every area of his brain. The scan also shows areas filled with water - not anything to be worried about - it happens to us all, as we grow old and is a sign of wastage. Old people! Alistair is only 12 months!

I am afraid this means Alistair will probably understand nothing and not be able to do anything, but the brain is still a mystery and other parts might take over.

I kept saying, "But Ali understands and, can do things. He hears the sounds of running water. He gets excited when about to have a bath..." But all the examples I brought up, he explained away. I asked him if he would mind telling my husband what he had just told me; giving him the chance to ask questions about his son. Strangely enough, John brought up the same examples that I had. Listening to the results of the scan a second time it seemed more alarming. While we understood he had brain damage, to hear the consultant say our son had 'total devastation of the brain' was hard to listen to. His excitement at bath time, recognising his brother, reacting to different situations; this surely should prove the consultant was wrong! He not validating our examples made us determined to prove him wrong; believing in our hearts, we were right.

Looking at the consultant's face, which showed so much compassion, we voiced our appreciation for all his help and wondered if he could offer us additional support. He said the hospital had an assessment centre attached to it, which he believed Alistair would benefit from. We cheered up as the consultant introduced us to The Paul Sandifer Centre Manager, while he excused himself, as he had surgery to attend to and people waiting. I looked at my watch. The consultant had spent two hours, patiently answering our questions.

The centre manager showed us around and explained the service. We were excited to hear that physiotherapy, occupational therapists and other team members would help develop a treatment plan, tailored to Alistair's needs. They would also help support us as parents. I wondered how much support we would need. We were both still, reeling from the news.

Our first impression of the centre was it reminded me of a playschool, with the addition of a soft play area, and a ball pool. It looked like a lot of fun; we knew Richard and Alistair would enjoy this. I spoke to other mums who told me how much the centre had helped them. We felt reassured and agreed to his starting. The team was eager to start the assessment process straight away. I could not wait to get back to the security of our home and wished I could wave a magic wand, back to when Alistair was five weeks old, with no sign of brain damage. We conceded to a full week's admittance for assessment the following week.

YES, TO JOYCE AND JEAN

I came home with John that night, both needing each other at this difficult time of our lives. The next day I travelled back to the centre to bring Ali home. Rather than go straight home, I decided to pop in on a friend who was looking after Richard. I was surprised to see my other friends all sitting in the garden, taking advantage of the hot sunny day. Richard, I noticed was busy playing with their children. They asked how we had got on and at first, I was reluctant to tell them but eventually, I came out with it. They sat stunned in silence, and I was conscious I had spoilt their beautiful day.

On the way back to my house, I would normally stop near the top of the hill, admiring the view. This day, as I walked up the beautiful hill, the sun had gone in, and blackness grabbed me. Tiredness overwhelmed me. I wished I could go to sleep and wake up from a nightmare; as if it never happened. I acted like this for the next few days - in denial, but every time I lay down, the same instructions came, "Go and see Joyce and Jean!"

Two days later, Joyce and Jean came to our house to find out about Alistair's scan results. I do not remember if I told them the truth, but I do remember anxiously saying, as they left, "I would like to come to one of your meetings." To my delight and apprehension, they said they would pick me up later that night at 8 pm. I did not have time to change my mind as the rest of that day swept by. Alistair seemed fractious and Richard played up, so I felt a sense of relief just to go out, leaving the children with John.

It disturbed me when Jean said, "Do not worry if you reckon they are all mad when you get there. The first time I attended, that was my impression." Driving to the meeting, we nearly collided with someone on their bicycle and one of them said that the near-miss was to stop us from going. By then, I was apprehensive of what could happen as I recalled John's warning about religious organisations ripping people of their money.

YES! TO JESUS CHRIST

We pulled up outside a terraced house, which I later found out belonged to a little old lady called Gladys. We entered it through a back room, bursting with people. I'd never seen so many people in such a small space. People sitting on the floor and chairs; others sitting on the stairs and to my relief, someone got up giving me their space on the settee.

My first impression was that everyone seemed so happy and welcoming. Someone gave me a praise book and by the time I found the song, they were onto the next one. Glad about Jean's warning; I looked around and noticed some people with their arms up in the air and others dancing. As I looked at the praise book, I was astonished to discover songs about healing and restoring sight to the blind. I read the life-giving words and experienced a sense of hope. A silver-haired man stood up and quietness reigned as he suggested it would be a good idea if people shared their testimony. I wondered what he meant by 'testimony'.

Astonished, I listened. Jean and Joyce must have said something about me, I thought. Then I realised I had never mentioned my experience at the Billy Graham meeting in London with my friend. Looking back, I did not realise the words I spoke back then had invited Jesus into my life. I remember my friend kept asking me if I had experienced a difference. Disappointed with my reply, she eventually gave up on me. Now, the people sharing their testimony had also attended a Billy Graham meeting and given their lives to Jesus.

Someone sang in a funny language; it was so beautiful! I remember wondering if this is what angels sounded like; I did not want the meeting to come to an end. I later discovered they called this language 'tongues'. Then the silver-haired gentleman stood up again, and said, "Is there anyone here who would like to ask Jesus into their life? if so, come to the front-room for prayer."

There seemed to be a rocket under me that propelled me up and out of my seat! I stumbled over people's legs to get to the front room. The *silver-haired gentleman*, whom others called Arthur, asked me what I wanted prayer for. I wanted 'their Jesus' in my life. Again, I mentioned being a Catholic. He explained that many people ask Jesus into their lives and being a Catholic did not matter. He asked me a few questions. He talked about Jesus dying on the cross for me and taking away my sins: having paid the price. It sounded so different from my previous experience as a Catholic, dreading confessions. For penance, I would have to say at least five Hail Marys and five Our fathers and would still not feel forgiven. Arthur instructed me to repeat a prayer after him. Joyce and Jean, with big grins on their faces, moved behind me as I repeated…

> *Lord Jesus, I want to know you, for me to be truly a part of your family.*
>
> *Just as I am I give myself to you. I am not perfect. I have done lots of things wrong as a sinner.*
>
> *Jesus Christ, I believe and trust in you. I believe you died for me. I give you all my sin, guilt and failure. Thank you for forgiving me. Thank you for making me clean. I give myself to you, holding nothing back. I give you all I have and all I am. Come in now, as*

my King and Saviour forever. Take charge of my life. Fill me with your Spirit. Make me what I should be.

Thank you, Jesus Christ. Amen.

As I repeated the words, I began to sway sideways. "It's his hands resting on my head, he's pushing me over!" I thought. Then the swaying stopped. He prayed for an extra blessing called the Baptism in the Holy Spirit; he explained I might find funny words coming through. "Just repeat them," he said. I liked this idea, still remembering the beautiful words I had earlier. As he prayed for me in a funny language, strange words formed in my mind. I repeated them; it sounded like the play-language I used with my sisters - a language no one else understood, apart from us. "Shalom, Shalom..." I kept getting the same word and repeated it. Again, I started swaying but was reassured by Joyce and Jean standing behind me, as I sank to the floor.

I told John all about the meeting and mentioned that no one had asked for any money. A few days later, whilst telling a friend about my recent experience as I made coffee for us, I started to shake. I shook so much, it stopped me from making the coffee. Then a warm and wonderful feeling of being wrapped in love enveloped me. She said my face radiated and pumped me for information about the meeting.

I was so happy. I found myself enjoying the children and all the demands Alistair made. Nothing seemed hard anymore. Everything seemed different. Life had seemed like hard work before but suddenly, it did not seem to matter, and every day seemed full of happiness. Yet, Ali was still up for most of the night and it was still difficult to feed him while Richard was as energetic as ever.

John liked the change he saw in me and encouraged me to attend the meetings. At one meeting, I also had my hands held up high in worship. I also went around telling everyone I meet, about Jesus. Many realised that Jesus loved them too and attended the fellowship meetings.

CLOUD NINE TO SQUARE ZERO!

Three weeks later, I turned down an invitation by a friend to go with her to see a fortune teller. She pleaded with me to go with her. I soon swallowed my misgivings, careful not to say anything to Jean or Joyce but deep down, knowing they would not approve. I explained it away, saying, "I'll go this once, and I'll sit outside." On the way there, I had this funny feeling in my tummy - now I believe it was the Holy Spirit, warning me not to. I told my friend I would wait outside but when we got there, I suddenly found out, it was me the fortune teller wanted to see first. As I waited outside, she told me how she had helped the police with finding a lost boy. I thought, "She can't be that bad if the police use her. It would not harm me if I go in."

When I entered the room, it seemed ordinary; no crystal ball but still I was fearful and wanted to run out. She held my hand telling me things about the children. But every time she tried to tell me something about the future, I turned her offer down. She kept saying there was a silver-haired man who had great influence over me. I thought, "Oh yes, my driving instructor." All the while as she talked, my head throbbed so bad; I could hardly hear what she was saying. By then, she must have realised I was resisting her and probably wondered why I was paying to see her. She offered to pray for the headache. I thought, "Others have prayed for me in the past so, the fortune-teller's prayer will do me no harm."

When she placed her hands on me and prayed, my head felt as if someone had split it open with an axe! When I came out it surprised me to hear that I'd been in there for a whole hour and a half, while my friend had been in and out within much less time! My friend excitedly described her experience on our way home, but I had lost my peace and joy, and hardly heard what she was saying.

Later that night, as we drove to the meeting Joyce and Jean noticed I seemed different. I told them I'd been to a fortune teller, which troubled them.

"You must have a word with Arthur," they said. By then, I realised he was the silver-haired gentleman the fortune-teller had referred to. He prayed for me and came against the fortune-telling spirit. My joy returned, but not the lovely, peaceful feeling I had earlier enjoyed. A measure returned, which I accepted and thought, "Well, I still feel much better than I used to."

MORE HELP FOR ALISTAIR

Life settled into a pleasant pattern, as Alistair was now attending The Paul Sandifer Centre at Great Ormond Street, every Friday. The first time we travelled in a volunteer's car, we had to stop twice as Richard suffered from travel sickness. My thoughts were, "How on earth am I going to manage this if he is sick each time we travel?" The driver was none too happy about it either. He was so pale by the time we arrived. This mode of travel was a one-off occurrence, and I had been nervous for no reason.

The NHS withdrew the car, as it was cheaper for them to provide an ambulance to take us to the station, and then another ambulance to meet us in the station, at the other end. The local ambulance men sometimes flashed their siren on and I would explain to Richard that it is normally only put on when there is an emergency. This used to make Richard feel special, and he loved going in the ambulance.

Whilst at the centre, Alistair had his physiotherapy and I would see the consultant. Sometimes, I waited outside his room for hours. It was always a relief to see him and at times they altered his epileptic drugs accordingly and monitored him closely as he was on a high dosage of drugs for his age. Too high a dose could cause sleepiness and lethargy while long-term use, could affect his health. The consultant had to keep adjusting Ali's medication to find a balance between life-threatening, Grand mal, epileptic fits and normal quality of life. At the centre, the occupational therapist showed me techniques on how to cope with Alistair's tongue-thrust. As soon as a spoonful of food went into his mouth, his tongue-thrust spurted the food out. I was taught to hold my thumb under his chin, with my fingers under his lower lip. The therapist did it with ease, but I discovered it was not as easy as she made it look. While trying to keep Ali's hands down, stopping him from smearing the food everywhere and holding the spoon, more came out than went in. It took an hour to feed him. When all the other mums would have finished and had lovely, clean little bundles, I'd still be ploughing on. A specialist corner high-chair was supplied, and it made a difference: like driving a manual car to an automatic one.

After dinner came physiotherapy, which Alistair strongly objected to for the whole hour, and made up for what he could not do, by yelling loudly. The day came, when he no longer cried in protest and cooperated with them - what patience they had! He was coming up to two years as they tried their hardest to get him to sit up. He would for a second, then go into spasm and topple over, with no balance or saving reactions. There were times I wanted to snatch him out of their hands as they seemed to push him so hard, and he would end up in tears. Richard did not like watching them 'hurting Alistair' and would play up for attention. I was eventually asked not to bring him. I was left torn between choosing what was best for Richard and what was right for Alistair - what a dilemma.

On one hand, Alistair needed physiotherapy and input as much as possible. He also had weekly appointments to see the consultant every Friday. Plus, Paul Sandifer's advice was making our lives much easier, but on the other hand, Richard needed to play with his friends and run around. None of which he could freely do, on a Friday. I prayed for the Lord to show me what to do. After discussing it with John, we both decided for the present time, that Alistair must come first as his life was at risk. I felt guilty about leaving Richard from 9.30 am to 5 pm. I never had a problem with finding people to have him, and since he seemed to enjoy being left, the guilt eased. By then, he was at a playschool in the mornings and I would have to rush down the road with both boys, drop Richard off, and rush back up the hill with Alistair, praying that the ambulance had not arrived early - leaving us behind.

CHAPTER 5

HEAVENLY EXPERIENCES

Heavenly Experiences!

Imagine my surprise when the doctor said, "You are at least eight weeks pregnant, Mrs Hubbard!" I did not expect John to welcome the news, as we had both been stretched to our limits with Alistair's needs. Plus, we were concerned that Richard was not getting enough quality time.

As early as twelve weeks into the pregnancy, I experienced difficulties. On my second visit to the antenatal centre, I was referred to see a consultant, due to my previous miscarriages. After taking the routine blood tests, the results showed I had low oestrogen and iron levels, as well as low blood pressure. On top of that, the baby was not putting on weight. All this accumulated in me being admitted into Gravesend Hospital, for 'bed rest'.

John's mum came to the rescue and moved in, to take care of Richard. We appreciated it would be asking too much of her if she had to look after Alistair too. Fortunately, Alistair was at the time receiving help from monthly weekend respite-care at Preston Screens, on the Isle of Sheppey. He loved it there. After hearing of our dilemma, they agreed to look after him whilst I was in hospital.

Rest in the hospital, I must admit, sounded inviting but the maternity ward being 'a restful place' was a joke: reflecting my ignorance, as this was where mothers were induced to off-set their labour. The other mothers-to-be laughed about this, as we were all meant to be on 'bed rest'. In the afternoons, our activity was to make teddy bears out of felt kits but there were only so many Teddy bears one could own. So, I asked for the surplus bears and started a cottage industry of selling them to the new mums. We aimed to raise money towards new equipment for the maternity unit at the hospital. This was difficult to do while on bed rest, so I utilized my refusal to use a bedpan, as my escape-time to get orders from new mums. Then I enlisted the nurses to do the distribution and collect the money. This helped with getting me through my boredom.

Visiting time remained the hardest experience. By the time John got home from Bromley and got washed, we were left with barely 15 minutes to spend together. Then my neighbour's children caught measles, which put my friends Joyce and Jean out of bounds from visiting me. My mother-in-law was also busy looking after Richard, while my brothers and sisters were scattered all over the country. During the afternoon-visiting time, I used to hide under the bedclothes and cry. I was full of thoughts that no one liked me, and void of friends. Talk about wallowing self-pity!

Later, my family informed me they were oblivious of me being in hospital. Both John and I thought the other had informed them. When my brother Gavin found out, he came to visit whilst on a business call in Kent. I was in stitches as he jokingly described a machine, he sold which helped with the delivery of babies. He described how on one follow-up visit, the client had altered the settings and calibrated the instrument too high, resulting in the doctors having to catch the babies, as the mothers gave birth. I knew he was exaggerating, but it made me, and all those listening to our conversation, laugh. I cheered up after his visit.

Soon after my brother's visit, the hospital released me home, to return only for weekly check-ups. Back at home, I found adjusting difficult after being in hospital for over six weeks. I was careful not to pick Alistair up too much. I was scared it would bring on a bleed. Alistair appeared withdrawn, after such a long separation. It made me feel guilty and it took lots of cuddles and reassurance before he came out of his shell. Richard, on the other hand, was delighted to have me back but missed his Nanny.

Once the nausea stage passed, I could feel the baby kicking. The hospital was pleased with how the pregnancy had progressed, aside from two frightening times of premature labour, but each time, they managed to stop it. As a precaution, they decided to insert stitches which would keep the womb from dilating. I was about six months pregnant at this stage.

The procedure went well, and I was transferred to a side-ward for monitoring.

HEAVENLY EXPERIENCES

I remember lying awake, feeling odd as a nurse took my pulse. I recalled peering down at myself lying on the bed. I thought I looked peaceful and speculated if I had died. Then an angel dressed in white, with massive wings, stood in front of me and said, "Come with me." Soon we were travelling fast up, what appeared like a large, open tube. Lights flashed passed us at great speed, with the angel ahead of me, holding my hand. We halted at a drab, gloomy-looking, eerie cavern. I saw flames in the distance and heard cries, which gave me the shivers and thought, "Oh! I hope I'm not going there!"

The angel seemed to understand my anxieties and we started to ascend again but at a slower pace. Now I found myself above the flames but though we were a long distance away, I could still feel the heat. I noticed bodies of people, in a fierce fire. They appeared not to die from the fire but remained in everlasting torment. I heard people crying out, long horrible yells of pain. The angel seemed to be making a point that I received, thinking; I never want to go there. I was relieved when the pace became faster and we geared swiftly away from the scene.

We came to a slow stop. Now in a place full of dazzling brightness, where there seemed to be life, within the colours of the light as I made out all different shades of white. Someone spoke, and I could perceive a figure, but it was too bright to see. Was it Jesus or Father God? Then Jesus introduced himself, telling me his name. I said, "I don't want to die. You promised I would see Alistair healed, and who will look after him?" In front of me appeared a panoramic movie of John, married to another woman, holding Alistair. John looked content. I was not happy about this. "You promised I would see Alistair healed."

He replied, "You have a choice before you make this decision. Would you like to visit heaven?"

Jesus appeared to read my mind as I thought, "Yes! Who would not want to see heaven?" He walked with me towards large, high gates. I noticed how the iron-work seemed lace-like in appearance. Two angels stood beside them and opened the gates at Jesus' command. As I entered through the gates, I immediately stepped into a garden and felt an encompassing sense of peace. The peace flooded every fibre of my being, causing me to think, as well as feel, that I had nothing to care about in the world. It was a sense of peace beyond my understanding. I wanted to stay there, so I stood still and did not move in case it stopped.

I glanced around and spotted, in the middle of the garden, a flowing, golden river - beautiful and vibrant - besides it, were coloured flowers. Everything seemed to be alive. I walked tentatively on the grass as it bounced back in shape. I was so, so tempted to stay; basking in the immense peace. There was such a struggle going on inside of me. With no more anxieties, I could stay and enjoy this peace. Yet I could hear a louder voice in my head shouting, "What about Alistair!" To my surprise, I heard myself say, "You promised I would see Alistair healed."

In a flash, as those words came out of my mouth, I found myself transported out of the garden, to another place. Also dazzling bright, I could make out movements of what I thought were angels. I saw other people there, dressed in white. I had an impression of a figure seated. Was it a throne? There was a lot of activity and singing all around the throne, but silence reigned the moment HE spoke.

His voice carried great authority, gentility, kindness, and love. "You have answered well; you have not yet done the work I assigned to you, which only you can do." Then he proceeded to give me a glimpse of my future, speaking of incredible things which to me, sounded amazing. I thought he had the wrong person, as the task sounded so far-fetched. I couldn't envisage healing thousands of people and causing a difference in people's lives, let alone travelling to the nations. The rest I do not remember.

The next thing I remember is being back on my bed, looking at my raised legs. I peered past my feet and noticed several doctors looking at charts. The doctors seemed surprised when I asked,

"What is going on?" The doctor in charge introduced himself and said, "You gave us quite a scare!" and explained about the nurse not discovering any pulse and raising the alarm. He asked me a few questions, seemed satisfied with my answers, and chuckled when I asked for a cup of tea. They lowered the bed and told me to press the alarm button if I felt strange in any way. As I drank my tea, I thought; it seemed hours I was in heaven. Yet, it could only have been a matter of minutes.

HELLO DANIEL!

After they inserted the stitch, the pregnancy settled down and there were no more false alarms.

Not until many weeks later. I had just sat down to relax before the babysitter was due to arrive when a gush of water-soaked my clothing. I rushed to the toilet, wiped myself and noticed fresh, red blood. I was horrified that my waters had burst and then to find that I was bleeding. I was startled and worried as I was only 29 weeks. Was that a contraction? I flinched with the pain as I called John. The babysitter agreed to stay with the children until John got back. I already knew the hospital routines well enough, with the earlier false alarms.

This time, I sensed something was different. Is the baby moving? Kick baby! Kick! We were both quiet as we made our way to the hospital; both remembering Alistair's early birth at 30 weeks. On arrival, the mid-wife, after a quick examination said, "We will wait for the consultant to examine you fully." The consultant arrived dressed in a dinner suit, with an expression which screamed, "Who has dared to interrupt my evening!" He sent John out of the room (who was much relieved) and examined me roughly, then exclaimed, "Oh my God! You are placenta previa!" and stopped examining me. I felt and saw more trickling-blood. His tone and words alarmed me; I was still in shock from the suddenness of the drama unfolding. "We are admitting you to Guy's Hospital for complete bed rest and monitoring. Although you are at risk, a good percentage of mothers with 'placenta previa' have gone onto have a healthy baby with a Caesarean Section. Guys Hospital has the expertise needed." It was the early hours of the morning. John and I were both apprehensive about the future. He tried to reassure me as he said goodbye, but it did not work.

Lying there, looking at the roof, listening to the ambulance siren and jolted by the bumps in the road, I tried to stay calm. The words of the consultant rang in my ear. As I prayed "Lord, let the baby be all right," I felt the baby kick and relief flooded me. I had two paramedics in the ambulance who joked with me between contractions. I was convinced as the ambulance took corners that I would fall off the stretcher. They told me they could not tighten the safety-strap any further as it needed to be loose around my tummy.

We arrived at Guys, where I was quickly reassured of the baby's heartbeat. Then they outlined a plan to see if drugs would stop the contractions. Otherwise, a caesarean would be necessary for my safety and that of the baby's. At this stage, I was rigged up to pain-monitor with strong contractions. The pain intensity was at ten, I was informed. The nurse told me, I had a high pain threshold - most people in her experience would have been using the gas or air as of then. The medication stopped the contractions, so the doctor decided to delay the caesarean for as long as possible, explaining that each extra week would give the baby a higher chance of survival. I must have fallen asleep afterwards, as I woke up in a room full of empty beds apart from one.

It was like a Ghost Ward - eerie and silent. The nurse sternly told me, when they realised I was awake, not to get out of bed and to stay as still as possible. She explained there was a high risk of bleeding and infection as my waters had burst.

It was difficult communicating with the other person in the ward, as she was on one end of the ward and me on the other. The only way through it was shouting as she shared her life story with me. This was her third baby, which she desperately wanted to keep. The other children, Social Services had taken away. Her last baby had been snatched away at two years old - she used certain vulgar vocabulary to express the injustice done to her. Someone had reported her for going out and leaving the child unattended. I told her about the time I had gone down to the local Co-operative leaving Alistair in bed, asleep. Every minute of delay by the lady at the till felt like hours. I never did it again.

She told me that her dad had abused her at twelve. When she found the courage to tell her mum about the abuse, she called her a liar and kicked her out. She described her fear of sleeping on the streets but in time, she had a gang who looked after her. Then, they turned violent and forced her into prostitution and drugs to survive. She described three back-street abortions that came with the territory of prostitution. She was proud that she now had a regular boyfriend. Both had stopped doing drugs for over three years and were looking forward to the birth of the baby. A week later, she got out of bed to show me the baby's clothes. Shocked to see they were worse for wear, I remembered my drawer at home, full of beautiful new baby clothes, and thought of giving her some.

The consultant was pleased with my progress, stopped talking about a caesarean and scheduled an ultra-sound. My last ultrasound was very early on in the pregnancy and now thirty-one weeks on, I was excited at this prospect. The ultra-sonographer showed me the pictures of the baby as she scanned my tummy. "Listen to his heartbeat - he has a strong heart." Then she stopped and whirled the monitor away from me. I could hear her on the phone asking for the obstetrician to come and have a look. She turned back to me and said she needed another opinion. "I believe there is something wrong with your baby. We will let you have the results as soon as possible." She said. My mind tried to catch up with the implications, whirling with fear.

They rushed me into the theatre and realised they were too late to do a caesarean. I could hear my friend screaming profanity in the next room. My contractions were steady and strong, and they gave me gas and air as I needed them. The obstetrician said, "This baby is in a hurry, we need you not to push until we are ready." Which proved difficult to do, but with the help of a lady doctor, I panted and then I was allowed to push. I pushed with all my strength and felt my baby come out. Then silence.

When the baby cried, it was such a relief. I noticed there was a strange atmosphere in the room. There was stunned silence apart from a shriek cry from the baby. "You have a boy." They said and took him away. I lay there thinking, "Any minute soon, I will hold him." But time ticked by.

When the lady-doctor came over and took my hand, I noticed she had been crying. The obstetrician joined her, and he too looked sad. "I have bad news; we do not think the baby will survive as he has an incomplete stomach." They could operate, but the chances of survival were slim as he was only 1lb 10 oz. "If he survived, he might only live for another few days or at most, weeks. I also notice you already have a disabled son, what is his name…? Alistair. And we spoke about his needs for a while. With the level of care, your baby will need and the countless operations as he grows, we do not believe you could cope with another disabled child. It sounds cruel, but we have another baby waiting for admittance, who has a stronger chance of survival. So, we have decided not to resuscitate your baby if he stops breathing." My worst nightmare had become a sudden reality. I looked at her wondering if he was waiting for me to agree with him.

She handed me the baby wrapped in a blue blanket; he was so small. I noticed a mop of bright red hair and wondered where he got that from. His little lip was trembling as he stared at me with bright blue eyes. Then I realised his lips were trembling and his blanket was now soaked in blood. The whole time the lady-doctor was talking about how beautiful the baby was. I told him how much we loved him, and his brothers would be excited to meet him. Then I stopped mid-sentence, realising they would never get to meet him. I hugged him until he died, living for only a few hours. The lady doctor took him off me; I did not want to let him go.

My arms felt empty, longing to hold him again. I saw someone approach me, not dressed in surgical gowns and wondered who it was. I checked again and saw the lady-doctor attending to the baby with the obstetrician and others. I looked again through a mist of tears... Was it? Jesus? He was a distance away from me, standing still and looking. Like the pictures, I had seen in books - white robe, tied with a cord around his waist. It was his eyes full of compassion and love that drew me. He came closer and I thought, "Am I really seeing this?" Then he stood right beside me and said, "You will be a mother to many and you will have many children." Then he walked away vanishing, as I watched.

DANIEL LIVES ON

The Obstetrician came over and asked, "Would you agree to the baby's organs being used for transplants?" The vision of my baby being cut up caused me to shudder in horror and responded with a firm "No." Now, every time I see documentaries or true stories about organ transplants, they remind me of how someone's organs, such as the eye, can give someone else the joy of seeing again and people who after a heart transplant can run with their children and have a normal life. I knew our baby's death could have helped many people by giving them a chance of a different life.

Recently, I was able to use this experience to help a friend when faced with the same decision about her mother's organs. The quickness of her decision enabled the doctors to use as many organs as possible, enabling others to have a chance of a different life. Signing up for a donor card is so easy and it helps family members to know your wishes, in case of death.

The hospital gave me my own side-room. Is this what a broken heart feels like? I wondered. My heart felt as if it had been stabbed, as I relived the warmth of my son within my arms and the wrench on my insides as the doctor took him from me. I noticed the sheets were soaked with my tears, but I didn't care. I wanted to die. I wanted to be with my baby. These thoughts were still heavy on my mind when I heard singing outside my room. My curiosity was aroused, so I sat up and noticed, through my open door, a woman with a mop, cleaning the corridor. Her singing was beautiful; I recognised the song as one we sang at my fellowship. I tried listening to the words, which I found soothing. I dried my eyes.

My room was her next port of call. When she came in she picked up a picture of my two boys. I was puzzled and wondered where the picture had come from. Then, I recalled grabbing it before we left the house for Gravesend Hospital. The nurse must have unpacked it, putting it on my bedside drawer. I heard the cleaner say, "How blessed you are to have two beautiful children!" Her words penetrated my sorrow. "Yes," I replied. "I am blessed." Then thinking, "She is right. I am blessed to have two healthy children. Many people don't have any - I am blessed." After cleaning my room, she left: leaving me with an unusual peace, which flooded me, as I fell asleep, exhausted.

I thank God the doctor had not taken my organ-donor response as final. This time, it was the consultant and his team who came in to see me. He apologised for not being there at the birth, saying, "You probably heard why..." Then I remembered hearing my friend's profanities as she gave birth. He agreed that I had been through a terrible ordeal and he was sure I wanted no other woman to go through what I had. One way to benefit from the baby's death, he recommended, would be to use his body for research to avoid future mishaps. What the consultant said made more sense, and his explanation appealed to me. So, John and I agreed that our child's organs be donated to help ease the pain of others. I signed the paperwork.

John asked about the burial and they said after an autopsy report the baby's body would be ready for burial and they would pay for the funeral. The reality of my baby's death hit me as he mentioned a funeral and that got me crying again.

Soon after, Richard came to visit. Standing at the end of the bed, he looked quite grown up for a little three-year-old. "I would have liked another brother and I am sad, but I have Alistair." He had said. He jumped on the bed and gave me a big hug. I smiled, thinking about how blessed I was to be the mother of two healthy boys.

NO TO PURGATORY!

The next day, two nuns came to visit, knowing from my medical records I was a Catholic. They worried me when they informed that the baby would stay in purgatory unless he was baptised. They kept on about this until I asked them to leave. I lost all my peace and kept imagining the baby stuck in purgatory - which sounded almost like hell - from the way they described it. Part of me said they were wrong, but all my Roman Catholic upbringing reminded me there was a purgatory.

John did not know what hit him when I phoned in great distress, telling him what the nuns had said. He calmed me down and said he would arrange for the baby to be baptised but did not know how to go about it. We agreed on the name 'Daniel'. That night, visions of the baby stuck between heaven and purgatory flooded my mind. I slept fitfully and could not concentrate on anything.

The nurse looking after me was so concerned; she suggested I went and saw my friend and her new baby. On my way to her bed, I congratulated other people on the new babies they were holding. I met a lady who had just given birth. Next to her was her daughter holding her new baby as well.

I was genuinely pleased for them but when I arrived at my friend's bed, seeing her holding her child, I silently thought, "Why did my baby die, when hers will most likely go into care!" I immediately pulled myself together, feeling guilty about my thoughts and quickly prayed; nothing of the sort will happen! Her baby girl was gorgeous, but I declined the offer to hold her. When she asked what I'd had, I forced back the tears and decided not to spoil her delight by shifting the conversation to her birth. We laughed over the profanity I had heard during her difficult birth, which cheered me up. By the time I got back to my room, I was dripping milk - another reminder of my loss.

Worried about my wellbeing, I later found out that John had phoned the local vicar who agreed to baptise Daniel by proxy.

After a few days, I was released home with instructions of bed rest, as a portion of the placenta had remained inside my uterus after the premature birth. They warned me I would get stomach cramps, which would help my uterus expel the placenta. Even though I had been warned, I was still frightened when I passed big chunks of blood. The local doctor reassured me it would soon stop while the midwife came to check on me each day. We both found it awkward, and her visits reminded me of how different life could have been. I did my exercises as instructed, and once my tummy returned to normal, neither she nor the doctor visited again.

QUARANTINED

Shortly after this, out of the blue, I was visited by an environmental officer dressed in protective clothing and looking like a spaceman. He explained that whilst in Guys, concern had been raised about my stools having an abnormal colour. They had been sent to the laboratory for investigation. I had excreted yellow stools and the nurse had commented on it, asking me about any recent holidays. Seeing the environmental officer that day jolted my memory on why I had been isolated while at Guys Hospital. He informed me they were taking the investigation further as a precaution, and he needed a stool sample from every member of my family. My room was now full of masked people in protective white clothes and rubber gloves.

He explained, "for your safety and that of others, you will be in-house quarantined until we have analysed your stool samples." To be honest this information did not bother me. It just gave me further reason to be depressed - it could not have gotten any worse. After the investigation, John and Richard were cleared but it turned out I had a type of salmonella, which meant I could receive no visitors until my stools were cleared

My doctor prescribed an antibiotic to help clear up any infection. This process took several weeks, and I also had to answer countless questions. Once they were reassured, I did not work in a restaurant or cook food for the public, I was also cleared of being a danger to others. Their prodding questions and research narrowed the salmonella-carrier down (in my memory) as a nurse who had examined me on her first shift back from a holiday in a high health-risk country. She had told me I was her first patient after returning from vacation.

When my friends finally came to visit, I was surprised at how vividly I could relive every moment of Daniel's birth: even about seeing Jesus. I was flat and empty by the time they left. It was as if the colour had gone out of life. I lay in bed with thoughts about John not wanting the baby as he had not even cried. Maybe he does not love me anymore. I would be better off leaving him before he leaves me. These thoughts invaded my mind repetitively. I would lay in bed hearing laughter downstairs - believing my own family did not care about me.

When it was time for Daniel's funeral, John went on his own as I was still on bed rest. It was just him and the vicar. My mother-in-law stayed back to look after Richard. John hardly spoke about our son's burial upon his return. All he said was how much he appreciated the vicar and his kind words. Guys Hospital was true to their promise. They had arranged and paid for the burial.

It was Alistair's social worker that shook me out of my depression and self-pity when he paid an impromptu visit. After saying, "We are putting Alistair on a care-order for him to be able to stay at Preston Screens longer." The words 'care-order' made me angry and panicky. I demanded they brought Alistair back home the next day. The social worker apologised and explained, "This is the only way Preston Screens can keep Alistair there any longer." They had thought it was what I wanted, he told me. I told him otherwise. My mother-in-law also joined in and he quickly left.

With Alistair back at home, I had no choice but to cope. I phoned the social worker's boss in anger and said they needed to rescind the care-order and he assured me, they would. I also asked for another social worker.

Alistair hardly smiled and did not react to us once he was back home. It took a few weeks before he allowed us to cuddle him. When we investigated, it turned out he had also been quarantined and his isolation consisted of being on his own, apart from when they fed and changed him. His careers also had to wear protective clothing for the whole time. To make his case worse, his quarantine went on for a longer period as Preston Screens had not been informed of the clearance. The damage to Alistair was clear, and I wondered how I would ever make it up to him.

NO TO SUICIDE

My friends encouraged me to attend a fellowship meeting with them. By then, the fellowship had moved into a new building. The idea appealed to me and I looked forward to it. To stop them from waiting for me and being late, I decided to drive myself, knowing how unpredictable feeding and putting Alistair to bed could be. Richard came with me as he enjoyed the singing.

We walked into a room full of happy people worshipping with hands raised and enjoying God. I stayed for a while, but I could not cope with their happiness; I wanted to scream. How dared they all be so happy when I was so miserable?

I grabbed Richard and ran to my car. While driving alongside the river, a thought popped into my head, "Why don't you kill yourself... All you have to do is drive into the river and it will all be over!"

I drove towards the river, knowing there was a steep drop on the other side. When I heard a sound from the backseat, I was suddenly conscious that Richard was also in the car. I thought about leaving him in his car seat at the side of the road, but the idea of a stranger finding him filled me with dread. I realised I couldn't allow that. I cried, knowing I needed help. The next thing I felt was a presence in the car. I felt someone sit in the front passenger seat but could see no one. Yet I knew someone was sitting there.

This Presence spoke, and as he did, I perceived the shape of a man. I wondered why I was not afraid. The Presence felt familiar. He asked me questions;

"Do you love your husband?" I thought about it and realised the answer was yes. As I said yes, the lies about our marriage seemed to fade away. "Do you believe your marriage could work and are you willing to work at it?" Again, I answered yes. Each time I answered yes to His questions, layers of lies dissolved. I found my hope rising as he asked more questions. Then the Presence said it would not be easy but if I worked at it, we would have a happy marriage. He said my husband loved me and had wanted the baby. He said He would bring deliverance to me and told me that I was not on my own.

On my way home, strangely, I felt almost happy and sensed the depression leave. Is that what He meant about deliverance? It was surreal, entering the house with Richard, as I realised things could have turned out so different. While the thought crossed my mind, I heard a voice in my head say, "All you have is on loan, to you." This pulled me up sharply, and I realised I should appreciate the gifts God loaned to me.

That evening, John and I sat having a heart to heart chat; forgiving each other. I learnt that I was wrong - he had been looking forward to having another child but believed I would die giving birth.

My selfishness hit me as he told me he had cried when the hospital phoned, informing him of the baby's death and how helpless he felt when I became upset about the baby being in purgatory. He talked about how hard it was telling Richard, his mum and our relatives of the baby's death. He then told me about the agony of having to register the baby's death and the actual funeral: the difficulty of watching the small coffin go in the grave and covered with earth. He said the vicar gave him some flowers to put on the grave.

My self-centredness hit me, once more, as we hugged and cried together. I told him how close I had been, to leaving him. I was drowned in my self-pity. He said he knew we could not go on the way we were. We laughed at our foolishness and kept our arms around each other, not wanting to let go; feeling closer than ever.

CHAPTER 6

DO I NEED DELIVERANCE?

Do I Need Deliverance?

Soon after being totally reconciled to John through forgiveness, I knew from my reading of the Bible that I would need deliverance from demonic interference and influence in my life.

Galatians 5:18-25 says, *"Now the works of the flesh are revealed, which are these: adultery, sexual immorality, impurity, lewdness, idolatry, sorcery, hatred, strife, jealousy, rage, selfishness, dissensions, heresies, envy, murders, drunkenness, carousing, and the like. I warn you, as I previously warned you, that those who do such things shall not inherit the kingdom of God. But the fruit of the Spirit is love, joy, peace, patience, gentleness, goodness, faith, meekness, and self-control; against such, there is no law. Those who are Christ's have crucified the flesh with its passions and lusts. If we live in the Spirit, let us also walk in the Spirit."* **NIV**.

Talk about *God's timing...*

As I recognised this need for deliverance, I heard from Joyce and Jean that a woman who specialised in deliverance was holding a meeting in a few days' time. We all decided to attend. The woman walked down the aisle, getting closer to me, all I wanted to do was run. The feeling subsided as we worshipped. Then she announced that she would normally ask people to come forward for deliverance at the end of her preaching but was prompted by the Holy Spirit to ask people to respond there and then. I responded.

As she laid her hands on me and prayed; I found myself on the floor, as if dead. I could hear her instruct her assistants, "Get her up, the demon is seeking to take her out. Spirit of death in the name of Jesus, I command you to leave right now!" I remember thinking, "What is she talking about?" She kept trying to deliver me, but nothing happened. She asked two of her ladies to continue praying for me outside, as she needed to carry on praying for others.

They took me into a ladies' cubicle where I sat on the toilet lid, squashed in with them: one at the side and the older, smaller lady in front of me. They prayed: ordering demons to leave. I laughed at the sight, believing it was comical - or maybe it was the demons mocking them. Still, nothing happened. Then I told them that I was seeing an image of a totem pole and asked if it had any relevance. I had a small totem pole at home. It was my pride and joy as my dad had given it to me as a youngster. He had also given me an oriental girl's costume. I used to imagine and dream of myself dancing around the totem pole and sometimes would see people from a faraway place, dancing around it too. The younger lady said there is an ancestral a spirit guide or a demonic influence attached to the totem pole. This alarmed me. "I don't want it, get rid of it!" I pleaded. Then I repented as she stood behind me, perched now on the edge of the toilet lid. Again, she ordered the spirit to leave and this time I felt bile in my mouth and the demons left with several big yawns.

Once I was back home, I wondered if I needed deliverance from witchcraft. Each year, my fellowship attended the Downs Bible Week, sometimes known as the Drowns Bible Week due to the season, as it often rained. Richard and I were sharing a tent with Joyce and her two children. I took the children to the meeting and Joyce stayed behind to cook our evening meal in the tent. During the meeting, I had a vivid picture of our tent being on fire. I ran out of the session to find this was the case, but Joyce had put the fire out with minimal damage. This disturbed me, and I fled to see my elder and asked for deliverance. He replied, "I do not think you require it, but I will pray about it." He came back and scheduled a date to pray for me.

DELIVERANCE FROM DEMONIC INFLUENCE

On the set prayer-day, I recall my two friends being there. I started by sitting on a chair but ended up making snake-like movements on the floor as they and the senior elders commanded all witchcraft to leave. Even though the elders prayed, commanding the demons to leave, they stubbornly stayed put. I then repented of seeking out fortune-tellers. I also repented of all forms of witchcraft and soon found my words stuck in my throat. Then this deep voice spoke through me. "She is mine! She is a queen of witches." Bewildered, I looked at my elder's face, but this outburst did not seem to bother him. Suddenly, my mind flashed back to the final chapter of *Dennis Wheatley's fiction, Occult Series* which had read, "Imagine yourself standing on the satanic star and read out loud, this prayer..." I had said the prayer.

My elder spoke with great authority but quietly, "She does not belong to you. She is purchased by the blood of Jesus. I command you to leave right now in the Name of Lord Jesus Christ and by the power of His shed blood." A sudden fury at Satan arose in me: *How dare he say I belong to him! I told him he was wrong as I belonged to Jesus and commanded him to get out!* I then repented of any ceremonies or words I had spoken and renounced the satanic prayer I had made. After a struggle, it left with the loudest scream which seemed to go on and on. *What will the neighbours think? Is this me screaming?* I had thought.

As I made my way to the car, I felt as though I was floating on air. My joy had returned! This continued, and others noticed the change. One lady came up to me, saying, "Why are you always smiling?" John noticed a difference too and encouraged me to go to church.

However, maintaining my freedom was a contest. Each night, my room was crowded with mocking-demons, taunting me. I could not see them, but I could hear what they were saying. Night after night, I would read my Bible out loud, not knowing what else to do. I would go to sleep pleading the blood of Jesus over me, saying, "I am covered by the Blood of Jesus."

One midnight, weeks after, I heard marching sounds, then a swooshing sound as if the air was being let out of a balloon. That night, the tormenting stopped, and I knew the demons had gone. I still believe, till this date, that the marching belonged to angels who had come to my aid; to deliver me.

As our church practised deliverance and many people came to the Elders for help to be set free, I had many opportunities to watch and learn all I could about deliverance and healing. Noticing my interest, they started to involve me in helping them.

DELIVERANCE FROM DEPRESSION & SELF-PITY

This time freedom came in a different form.

While relaxing and enjoying the sunshine I suddenly felt depressed and self-piteous, as my thoughts spiralled out of control. The first thought was *"poor Richard! He had missed out because of Alistair - not able to take him swimming and do other things he sees his friends do."* I then recalled how upset he had been, seeing his friends get in their cars, to go swimming. Then I thought, *"My friends had not offered to take him. They said they were friends but look how they treated*

Richard." My rational mind said they could not cope with Richard (being a non-swimmer) and their children, but the self-pity overtook this. After that, I recalled when their children had measles and did not come to visit me in hospital. Many other memories flooded my mind. My thoughts were horrible, taking me deeper and deeper into a black hole and almost sucking the life out of me. I wondered what was happening to my mind.

Then I remembered Derek Prince's book: *Baptism in the Holy Spirit*. It had been recommended for me to read so I ran upstairs to get it. I recalled receiving the Holy Spirit, but this book mentioned fire. I read the prayer at the end, asking for the Baptism in the Holy Spirit and fire. I read it twice: the second time out loud and suddenly, I was *sick*. It must have been self-pity that left me, as those thoughts never returned, and I no longer struggled with self-piteous thoughts.

Growing up, I had always viewed God as being synonymous with anger. The truth of him not being an angry God was also borne out of an experience, soon after my deliverance from self-pity. I had just bathed Alistair which was never an easy task because I had to hold his head up out of the water while washing him with the other hand. He was a nice smelling bundle on my bed. Then he had a petit mal epileptic fit and this caused him to be sick all over the bed.

I became extremely angry at God *and told him what I thought of Him* for not stopping Alistair's fits! As soon as I started, all my frustrations poured out. Once done, I sat in fear, believing I would soon be struck by God. *How dare I talk to God like this?* To my amazement, I heard Him say, in an audible voice, "About time too!"

SELF-DELIVERANCE by REPENTING

I learnt some truths about repenting as I read a book called *Emotionally Free* by Rita Bennett, who wrote about yet another type of deliverance, called Inner Healing. Some people refer to it as soul-healing, as peoples' souls (comprising our will, mind and emotions) were healed. As I read about these ladies who prayed for hurting-people, I would remember different instances in my life when I had been hurt as a child. The book affirms it does not always mean the parents were *bad parents*: although this is how the child would perceive it. It gave various testimonies which I could relate to as true experiences of God's transforming power. One man's experience had been about his father not being there for him. I made a connection and recalled how my dad worked until late and we hardly saw him, apart from the weekends and holidays. Yet, he did most of the punishing and we were often spanked by him. My perception of God was punitive - a god that was not there for me. One who was there to blame and punish me. As the Holy Spirit prodded me, I realised I needed healing in that area. I forgave my dad for not being there for me. One day, as I read my bible, I noticed God gave people, chance after chance to repent. At that moment, the lie that God was an angry, punishing-God left me. I began to pray and address Him as my Father. Before this, when people prayed to God as Father it would grate, thinking, "They should be praying to 'God', not to a 'father'!" But now I knew him, as 'Abba Father' and I could relate to him as a loving father also.

The Holy Spirit dealt with my unforgiveness, as I gave Him permission into the cellars of my life. I desired to have a pure heart. He brought up instance after instance, where I needed to ask forgiveness.

He flashed a memory into my mind, of standing in my friend's house feeling envious that her house was so tidy: *even having time to bake cakes for her husband.* Then he showed me other times, I had been jealous of people. One time, looking over the fence seeing my friends sunbathing, with my garden full of their children, which to be honest I did not mind but I remember thinking, *'It's all right for some!'* Then he took me back to times in my childhood where people had bullied or misunderstood me. I saw myself looking at my sister's new bike (as if it was happening then) which had been a prize from my parents for passing the 'Eleven Plus Test'. I witnessed myself resisting the urge to smash it up, as jealousy overwhelmed me. I was surprised at the depth of the jealousy, as I knew I loved my sister.

As I repented, Jesus showed me another memory of a circle of children who had surrounded me. One of the girls raised her fist to hit me. I had flinched, waiting for the blow; but nothing happened. I remember being surprised when they ran away (now back in the moment, I saw Jesus standing there) thinking that a teacher was approaching them. I realised He had stopped the girl from hitting me. He brought memory after memory back. Then He showed me any anger, resentment or other sins attached to each memory. I repented and asked forgiveness for my sins. In the end, I saw a picture of me standing in a circle holding hands with each of the people I had forgiven, with Jesus' arms outstretched behind as He encircled us, smiling.

Sometimes, the Holy Spirit would bring healing by showing me the truth rather than the lies. I remember thinking I had no friends at school; he displaced this lie by showing good memories when I had played with other children.

This inner healing went on for months.

I would send the children to school, after which the Holy Spirit would show me memory after memory; standing with me. Together we watched Alistair in the hospital, as the Holy Spirit reached my inner being, healing the trauma of watching Alistair as a little baby having fits in the hospital.

After months of teaching Alistair how to crawl, he finally scuttled across the floor. I was still celebrating this milestone when I watched with horror as his movements evolved into a massive grand mal seizure, resulting in hospital admission for a week. He never crawled again. On and off during the weeks, the Holy Spirit took me through my years of disappointment. Alistair started talking, then he stopped after another grand mal seizure: losing all words he had recently learnt. We noticed a pattern. Each time a seizure occurred, it appeared to wipe away any recent achievements.

FREE TO CRY AT LAST!

Going from one trauma to another, with no time to process it, I learnt to stuff down any emotions, believing I needed to be in control. Thinking, "If I am a crying mess, of what help would that be to doctors and others trying to help?" I also believed that if I cried, I would not be able to stop myself. I tried to deliver myself from this but without success. I asked my friends who had also read 'Emotionally Free' and now prayed for others, for help.

They prayed for me and asked the Holy Spirit to come. I renounced all spirits of control over my emotions and we all worshipped, not knowing what to do next. As I worshipped, I had such an experience of God's love for me. I started to cry. I knew, as I cried, the loss of Daniel was being healed and felt reassurance that I could stop crying. Much to my surprise, I hadn't gone mad and lost control.

I shared my healings with others, and soon, my friends and I had a steady stream of people asking for inner healing and we saw remarkable changes in people's lives. There seemed to be another pattern forming. When the Holy Spirit brought healing to a certain area of my life, within the same week, people in need of the same form of healing would visit. God was acting out his word. *"And we know that in all things, God works for the good of those who love him, who have been called according to his purpose."* Romans 8:28 NIV

I would have loved to say all my deliverance and inner healing were as smooth as that. I later discovered, that going to the spiritualist and allowing her to pray for me had given permission for more demons into my life. I recalled times I had hated myself so much that I had considered suicide by slashing my wrists as a child but didn't have the courage to do it.

As I read about deliverance and received it, I did not realise I would one day lead counselling and deliverance teams: that this was part of my destiny. I avidly read and listened to tapes about faith and deliverance.

CHAPTER 7

TAKE AUTHORITY!

Take Authority!

During the early stages of learning about deliverance, Alistair aged about three was admitted to the local hospital with an unknown cause of very high temperature. He was placed in isolation as a precaution. They told us that the next few days would reveal what was causing it. Tired and relieved to be home after being at the hospital all day, I looked forward to going to bed. I was surprised to hear the Holy Spirit say, "Pray now!" The urgency and authority in His voice startled and alarmed me. Panicky, I prayed not knowing what I was praying about but thought it must be about Alistair. These days, I would ask questions but then I had not received such a revelation to ask. The Holy Spirit interrupted my prayers and said, "No, I do not want you to pray like that, pray like this. I want you to rebuke the angel of death!"

My first thought was, "How on earth could I?" Then the Holy Spirit gave me an open vision of Alistair lying in his hospital cot surrounded by doctors working on him. An oxygen mask was over his face and to my dismay; I noticed there were two enormous oxygen cylinders in the room. There were doctors and nurses on either side of him. The scene was alarming, but I heard the Holy Spirit say, "Do not fear, the angel of death is asking for your son, I want you to rebuke it." At this, I saw this tall, black, menacing angel hovering over him.

The Holy Spirit led me on how to pray. I do not remember precisely how he instructed me to pray. He told me to take authority over it, in the name of Jesus; rebuking it away from Alistair and to apply the blood over Alistair. When I first followed those instructions, nothing happened; it was still there. Panic rising, I asked, "What do I do now since the prayer had not worked?"

The Holy Spirit read my mind and said, "You have the authority." He brought to my remembrance teachings I knew about the authority we have over principalities, powers, rulers and dominions of darkness. Rehearing the teaching, as if I was there listening to it, caused courage and boldness to rise within me. I got righteously angry. How dare this angel of death think he can try to take Alistair! This time, I instructed it to leave and saw it starting to withdraw on what unfolded like a screen, on my front room wall. It was like a movie. I heard doctors and nurses talking - all in colour. I could not hear what they were saying but could see the concern on their faces. My mind tried to compute the scene before me. Almost in a state of unbelief and unable to understand, though my spirit man was seeing and believing it. Still, the angel of Death did not go and now tried to intimidate me with its presence. It looked at me as if it could get me. I went cold inside. Once more the Holy Spirit urged me to tell it to go. Now feeling desperate, I had taken authority and done what I knew to do, I said, "Jesus help."

Take Authority!

I felt like I had grown into an empowered, spiritual giant-now bigger than the death angel. I pointed at the screen and with a great authority, which seemed to fill me and the room, demanded *it*, to leave: in Jesus' Name. Scriptures flooded my mind, and I repeated these and declared; the blood of Jesus covers Alistair and nothing by any means can harm him or me. "Get out, now! Go! In Jesus Name."

By then, I was shaking (as the adrenaline hit in) but became much relieved when it finally left, with a whoosh!

The Holy Spirit said, "Alistair will live." Peace descended on me, so much so, I decided not to telephone the hospital to find out if Alistair was okay, and I slept peacefully.

The next day, I went to visit Alistair, and his room was exactly how I had seen it in the vision. Cot pulled out, with two large tall oxygen cylinders beside him.

The reality that I had not imagined what had happened the night before was frightening but also reassuring. The seriousness of the situation was confirmed by his doctor, "Your son gave us a fright last night. We thought we were going to lose him. We will leave the oxygen cylinder there as a precaution".

This experience made me realise to an even greater extent, the authority we have in Christ's name and the power of his blood. The

Holy Spirit led me to learn about the work of His blood and how to apply it. There is power in the blood of Jesus!

FAITH INTO ACTION

Below are the Confessions I learnt to use when under attack. I also used them to help others find freedom from attacks:

> The Blood of Jesus overcomes and there is power in our testimony of what Christ has done in our lives, as reflected in Rev. 12:11, *"And they overcame him (the accuser of the brethren, the devil, the thief, Satan) by the blood of the lamb and by the word of their testimony, and they did not love their lives to the death."*
>
> **Redemption:** Through the blood of Jesus I am redeemed out of the hands of the devil.
>
> **Forgiveness:** Through the blood of Jesus all my sins are forgiven.
>
> **Justification:** Through the blood of Jesus I am justified, made righteous, just as if I never sinned.
>
> **Cleansing:** While I walk in the light as He is in the Light, the blood of Jesus Christ, God's son is cleansing me now, and continually from all sin. Through the blood of Jesus, I have been washed whiter than snow.

Life: Through the blood of Jesus I have Divine, Eternal, Resurrection Life, I shall never die.

Access: Through the blood of Jesus I have access into the holiest of all, into the immediate Presence of Almighty God my Father.

Intercession: The blood of Jesus sprinkled in heaven is speaking on my behalf, pleading continually for mercy.

The above confessions were made more alive to me after praying for a woman enslaved to the sin of prostitution. She had accepted Jesus into her heart, but she was not a churchgoer. When I finished praying, she said she felt clean: as if someone had washed her whiter than snow.

From the moment I recommitted my life to the Lord, the process of deliverance started. I seemed to be in his training school for spiritual warfare. He would remind me to put on my armour according to Ephesians 6:10. He introduced me to this by showing me a scenario in my mind's eye of two people: one had armour on, over his clothes; the other was just clothed. With a prowling large lion watching them, the Holy Spirit asked, "Who do you think the lion will attack?" I said, "The one without his armour." He said, "That is why it is important to put on your armour each day."

One day, many years later, after forgetting to put on my armour, I was under continuous attacks. I became frustrated, so I moaned to Father God about the situation. He gave me a vision of my shield of faith; it covered me from my feet to the top of my head, wrapped around the front of me. It was made of such bright metal that it dazzled the enemy. He showed me the demons, shielding their eyes and backing away. What a reminder to continue to put on the armour every day and how comforting to know my shield of faith is so bright, it dazzles the enemy! The interesting thing is, as this revelation became truth, the attacks stopped.

I have since made a habit of putting on my armour as I get out of bed. It also reminds me of who I am and whose I am.

For instance, I might pray it like this;

- Father, I put on the belt of truth, tight around my waist; let me be aware throughout this day, of whose I am and what You have done for me.

- I put on the breastplate of righteousness. Thank you for dying on the cross for me and making me in right-standing with you. Help me to guard my heart today; to be quick, to forgive.

- I put on the sandals to announce the good news of peace; guide my steps today. May I not miss

Take Authority!

opportunities to share your goodness and kindness today. May I carry your peace wherever I go today.

- I wrap around me, the shield of faith with which you will put out, all fiery darts of the enemy. Increase my faith and may I do your will this day. Your word says I can expect you to put out all the fiery darts of the enemy, sent at me, my family and loved ones, this day.

- I take up the helmet of salvation and I ask you to guard my ears and mind against the fiery darts of the enemy and increase my sensitivity to hearing the Holy Spirit and I put your cross and blood between me and any other voices, not of you.

- Continue to transform my mind and I take my thoughts captive and make them obedient to You. I pull down everything in my mind that seeks to exalt itself, higher than the name of Jesus.

- Lifting up your sword of the spirit (the word of God - I act this out practically) may I use it effectively with your authority and may you empower your word today…

I then bind to total inactivity, every principality, powers, rulers, dominions of darkness and unclean spirits working against me, my family, ministry, clients and clients' families. I bind and rebuke any strongman and the cohorts from working against me or anyone I am involved with by saying:

- I paralyse and scramble the languages in the first and second heaven. I cancel out every plan of the enemy made against me, my family, my loved ones, my clients, their families, Esther's for the Nations, every leader, member or anyone else I am involved with.

- I ask you, God, to paralyze all their evil forms of communication so they cannot communicate with their strongmen and cohorts.

- I cancel out any plans made during the night against me or my loved ones and I send those plans into confusion and disarray. I loose in God's plans for my day, his purposes, his destiny for my life and my family and others. Father, show me ahead of time the plans and devices of the enemy against me. Cover me and all my loved ones and sphere of influence with your blood. Send your angels to help me and my loved ones this day.

- Father, release all kinds of wisdom and understanding for this day, sharpen my discernment and hearing from you.

I round up by praying about whatever the Holy Spirit brings to mind, then I worship and thank him for who he is.

Basic warfare is to help keep us safe. Remember to embark on this, from a place of victory.

HEARING FROM GOD

I enjoyed sharing the revelations I felt the Holy Spirit was telling me, believing everyone heard from God in the same way. For me, it was having a two-way conversation. I expected him to answer, and he did. I was shocked and troubled when another Christian of longstanding said, "I do not believe it is God speaking to you. It sounds good, but Father God does not talk to me like that, I think you are being deceived."

I soon began to doubt the voice of the Holy Spirit and chose to believe this 'Christian of longstanding' that God was not speaking to me. In hindsight, I wonder why I never checked this out with others. The Holy Spirit still carried on speaking and I would tell him to go away and be quiet. At first, he persisted but eventually, the Holy Spirit went quiet. It was as if I had lost my best friend. I was overwhelmed with deep sadness and a sense of loss. After a while, I started talking to him like I used to, but nothing came back. Eventually, I believed (the lie) that 'He' was not interested in speaking to me and completely forgetting the silence was of my doing.

I asked others how they heard from God. Most said they heard God through reading the bible. I also remembered the times this had happened. Several times as I read the bible, the words would leap out of the page, come alive and speak right into a current situation:

giving me the encouragement and leading I needed. Often, these same words were of great help to others later, within the week.

During this time of silence, I read my bible at every spare moment. I would get the children ready for bed and grab my bible. When they watched their children's programmes, I would do my daily bible readings using 'Every Day with Jesus' by Selwyn Hughes. I saw that God continually spoke to people in the bible, starting in the Garden of Eden with Adam and Eve, then later on Noah: specifically instructing him on how to build the ark.

It seemed God was taking me on a journey through the bible. Showing me different people: Abraham, Samuel, Isaiah and Jeremiah and many others who had heard God speak to them. Abraham, I noticed, immediately obeyed God's instructions, though (this may have been easy for him because) he had been practising hearing God throughout his life.

I wondered how I would have responded if told by an angel of God to sacrifice my son. In Samuel 1, God spoke to Samuel. At first, he did not recognise God's voice. It was almost as if he was on the wrong frequency: hearing, but not recognising it was God. In the New Testament, Jesus had conversations with his disciples. The Holy Spirit brought God's message to Peter.

Acts 10:13-15 *"And there came a voice to him, Rise, Peter; kill and eat. But Peter said; Not so Lord; for I have never eaten anything that is common or unclean. And the voice spake unto him again the second time, What God hath cleansed, that call not thou common."*

I realised I had become so frightened of the supernatural and the thought of being deceived that I had believed the lie; I was not hearing from God. God speaks to us through his word, but he also communicates with our inner man, through the voice of the Holy Spirit. I repented of believing the lie, and immediately I heard the Holy Spirit say, "My sheep hear my voice." I later found this in John 10:27, *"My sheep hear my voice, and I know them, and they follow me."* I also read in Isaiah 55:3, *"Give ear and come to me, hear me that your soul may live."*

I was overjoyed that my relationship with the Holy Spirit had been restored, but soon realised he had never stopped talking to me. He just spoke using the bible, deepening my relationship with Him and His Word. In time, He showed me how to test the spirits behind what I hear, as there are deceiving spirits who masquerade as angels of light.

This is what I do according to 1John 4:1-16

I get them to repeat the prayer below:

I serve the Lords of Lords and King of Kings. Jesus Christ who was born of a virgin came to earth in the flesh, died on the cross, and rose from the grave three days later. This same Jesus, who is

> *God, sits in heaven on the right hand of the father; this Jesus is my Lord and master.*

Some say it word-for-word, others say it differently, but with the same meaning. So far, no one sent by God has minded me testing them and they often seem amused by sometimes adding on how much they love him.

Demonic powers normally say it, but don't get very far. They will not say Jesus Christ came in the flesh as 1 John 4:1-2 bears out.

> *"Beloved, believe not every spirit, but try the spirits whether they are of God: because many false prophets are gone out into the world. 2 Hereby know ye the Spirit of God: Every spirit that confesseth that Jesus Christ is come in the flesh is of God. 3 And every spirit that confesseth not that Jesus Christ is come in the flesh is not of God: and this is that spirit of antichrist, whereof ye have heard that it should come; and even now already is it in the world. 4 Ye are of God, little children, and have overcome them: because greater is he that is in you, than he that is in the world." vs 15 "whosoever shall confess that Jesus is the Son of God, God dwelleth in him, and he in God." (KJV)*

A year later, Father God continued my education on hearing his voice. One time, I really felt in my spirit, I had a prophetic word during the meeting at our church. All indications lined up, this would not have gone against the flow of the meeting or where the

Holy Spirit was taking it. Again, I asked Father God if he meant me to share this word and was surprised to hear a "No". I questioned this, and he said, "Why would I not want to give good gifts to my children." Afterwards, I realised he was teaching me to listen to his heart not just his voice.

God often speaks through others. I learnt to be open about listening to others, especially when they share his goodness and faithfulness. One time, I was in a sticky situation. While wondering what to do, it was as if I heard one of our leaders' voices and that of a friend's. It was as though they were next to me. I heard them advise me on what to do in that situation. The Holy Spirit would also bring scriptures to my remembrance. Since we continually learn from each other, we must be careful who we listen to. When I worked on a project for older people, I had the privilege of hearing many wartime stories of God's deliverance. Some did not realise it was God's deliverance at work. When I said to them, "That sounds like divine intervention," it made them think.

God speaks through nature. Another time was up in our woods, enjoying watching different trees bend and move to the rhythm of the wind. As I continued looking at them, I realised that each tree was individual. Some had thick trunks, others less, while saplings bent more easily but came back up quickly like an elastic band.

The Holy Spirit interrupted my thoughts. He said that each person receives my Holy Spirit in a unique manner. If I were to fill that sapling to the level I fill that tree with the thick trunk, it would overwhelm it. I know precisely what each person needs and give good gifts accordingly. I have never forgotten this encounter and see trees differently now - each with his own character and ways, just like us.

GOD SPEAKS THROUGH BOOKS

Books have been important in my walk with God. Maybe that is why I am writing one now. I am so glad there is such a rich resource of books to choose from. I love to read about people of faith: Rees Howells, Corrie Ten Boom, Kathryn Kuhlman, Reinhard Bonnke.

Among many books were:

> *Evicting Demonic Squatters and Breaking Bondages* by Noel and Phyl Gibson,
>
> *Pigs in the Parlour* by Frank and Ida Mae Hammond.
>
>> I learnt from these books that I needed to repent of hereditary bondage and dominations and discovered what the spirit-groupings were. I was no longer just casting out demons but getting to the

roots and causes of entry and learning how to do 'self-deliverance' on myself.

Commanding your Morning by Cindy Trimm is excellent.

Boundaries by Cloud Townsend has helped many of my clients.

The Five Love Languages by Dr Gary Chapman
Anyone can find out (online) what their love language is, by answering a few questions. This is a resource I would recommend to every Christian. I have witnessed marriages growing stronger, using this awareness tool. He has written also about children's love languages and his weekly blogs are resourceful.

Books on Prayer by Dutch Sheets helped me develop my intercession prayer life.

Love on its Knees by Dick Eastman encouraged me to pray for others.

Intimidation by John Bevere taught me about the spirit of intimidation with the opposite spirit of Might.

Hosting the Presence by Bill Johnson has particularly impacted my life positively. I build myself up in the Lord by listening to his CDs as I travel.

Transformation of the Inner Man and *Healing the Wounded Spirit* by John and Paula Sandford are helpful when praying for people

Breaking Bondages, by Quin Sherrer and Ruth Anne Garlock.

The Believers Guide to Spiritual Warfare by Tom White was one of the first books I read on spiritual warfare. It is easy to read, with a resource of prayers at the back. The one for children has been adopted by many mums I know.

Unwrapping Lazarus by Pete Carter (my senior pastor's book) had me in tears; it is such a faith-building book.

I had the privilege of spending time with Dutch Sheets and Dick Eastman, who both prayed for me. After prophesying over me, Dick Eastman sent his aid out and he gave me a copy of every one of his books for free. On one book, as he was signing it, he remarked, "I don't know why, but this book will be important for your future." It has been, but that is another story for the future.

After signing, he told me to take books for each of my intercessory team - how generous! He must have given us books worth way over a hundred pounds. I found Joyce Meyer books and tapes easy to read and listen to. Graham Cooke is a fountain of wisdom, especially around prayer, the prophetic and destiny. Derek Prince's books are timeless.

Soaking in God's word and resting in His presence, just loving on him, are the times God has often spoken profoundly. In these times I barely say anything other than "I love you, God." I do more listening than talking.

When we pray, it is easy to forget it is meant to be a two-way conversation. Father God loves to talk to us, and as he is all-knowing, he finds the best ways to reach us. Some of my friends just feel him, others have pictures, others just know he is there listening. He communicates often, and sometimes, we need to change our channels to hear him more.

SAVING MY MIND BY GIVING HIM ALL

About two years after Baby Daniel died, I woke up one morning, exhausted. I dragged myself out of bed, fed and dressed both boys on autopilot before they left for their different schools. I thought it would not hurt to go back to bed; have a rare snooze. My whole frame felt weighty as I pulled myself upstairs to bed. It seemed to take forever getting there. When I placed my heavy head on the pillow, my mind burst with images of the baby dying, as if it was happening at the moment. Like a movie playing in my mind (which I was unable to turn off) I was suddenly shown other traumas...

I am on the stretcher listening to the police siren, shaking with fear, as the police escort the ambulance to Guy's hospital. Twenty-eight weeks pregnant, trickling blood and in labour, my waters had broken. I switch to scenes of Alistair in hospital. His little body jumping in the air as he has repeat-fits while fighting for his life. He is okay one day, then critical the next. I shudder on the bed as I relive these traumas. Why is this happening? I remember being okay during those ordeals. In fact, I remember having no time to process the traumas before the next crisis developed.

I struggle to get up off the bed, but I cannot move - my legs feel like lumps of lead and my body seems too heavy to move. I feel drained and frightened, as I think about the boys and things I need to get done before they arrive home. But then, a part of me does not care. All I want to do is to sleep and not wake up. I shake and want to scream but I know that if I do, I may not stop. My mind floods with an overload of flashbacks, rolling in one after the other. Am I going crazy? What is happening? God, help me!

Then, the Holy Spirit said, "Give me your mind." Questioning why, since I had given him my life - surely this includes my mind? The Holy Spirit carried on, "You have not made me Lord of your life in your mind and other areas. I want all of you." Without being instructed on how; I just seemed to know what to do. In prayer, I gave Him my mind, my thoughts, my memories, my brain, even naming the parts of the brain I knew. *I continued, knowing he wanted everything.* I gave him my body, my eyes, my ears, my mouth, my speech and asked that they would honour him. I repented for not making him Lord of *every area*. I ignored the flashbacks and now intrusive thoughts. I pushed myself to continue Praying.

I moved onto our finances, our marriage, my friendships, our children, my husband, his job; thinking, "Surely, I must have covered everything." The Holy Spirit said, "What about your house, your car, possessions." and as I included them, I was reminded of even more things to add to the list. "Your worries, your anxieties, I want to be Lord in every area of your life." As I finished, I realised that my mind had stopped replaying horrible memories and there was quiet in my mind.

Yet, I still could not move and realised I needed help. I shuffled to the side of the bed and with tremendous effort, reached for the telephone and dialled my friend Jean. I pushed my distress aside as I tried to tell her what was happening. "I will be there in a minute."

Recently, I have wondered, how she got in. The front door was shut after saying goodbye to the children, and the back door remained locked from the night before.

Relief washed over me when she arrived. I told her through tears about the flashbacks, still shaking and wanting to scream. Peace overwhelmed me as she prayed, and the shaking stopped. I had no strength to argue when she said she was going to contact our doctor and my husband.

I recall little, other than the doctor saying "I am not surprised, you are not superhuman. You are experiencing post-traumatic distress - the shock has caught up with you." He gave me an injection and instructed me not to get out of bed for at least three days. He told me I was suffering also from exhaustion. "I stress, you are to do nothing, and I am subscribing after those three days - it might be longer - sun, fresh air and rest. I will visit each day for the next three days to monitor you. If you refuse to rest, you will end up in the hospital, but I believe if you take your medicine and take a rest for some days, you will make a full recovery."

My heart started sinking - recently my husband had told me how busy they were at work. I told the doctor this, but he said, "He has no choice, otherwise you would need to be hospitalised."

My enforced rest went on for a month; I remember not being able to make simple decisions. John once asked me what he should put in the sandwiches. My mind panicked at the prospect of trying to decide if cheese or ham. It seemed immensely important to get it right. If I made a wrong decision, it was almost as though life would end.

The doctor was correct. I recall one day while laughing at the children's antics. It was like a weight came off me. I noticed the warmth of the sun on my face as I watched Richard playing in the sand at the seaside. John's work had given him an immediate extra holiday when they heard of my state. The grey fog lifted, and colour came back into my life. I soon woke up looking forward to the days. Before, this it was an effort to do anything; working on remote, not feeling anything.

Looking back, I believe by giving God my mind that day, he stopped me from having a nervous breakdown. Also, God knew we needed the space to enjoy ourselves as a family. So often we think we have made God Lord of our lives, but we like to hold back on certain areas.

Why not ask the Holy Spirit if there are any areas you need to hand over to Him, today?

I regularly check that everything is His and seem to know; worrying is a sign that I have taken back the responsibility. I have discovered that the areas I hang onto, God cannot work on and when he has 100% of my life, it is also protection for me.

CHAPTER 8

AN OPEN DOOR FOR *'Annabel'*

An Open Door For 'Annabel'

As a child, I remembered having repetitive dreams of feeding the poor and seeing hands reaching out to me.

Three years after I became a Christian, my church asked me to get involved in praying for those who needed deliverance. As time went on, I realised, some people did not need this type of ministry. I noted they would be helped more by us listening and unravelling what was going on in their minds: discovering and touching on the many hurts and wounds related to their early childhood.

I experienced a steep learning curve when we embraced a young lady *'Annabel'* into our family. She taught me many lessons. We welcomed her into our home, and she joined us on holidays to help with Alistair. After a year, I felt as if I was being strangled whilst with her. The Holy Spirit showed me this as an 'octopus spirit', with many legs and suckers. One of its legs was wrapped around my neck, trying to strangle me; causing a feeling of powerlessness. He said, "It is seeking to control you."

I asked what I should do, aware I needed to repent of not establishing good boundaries for either of us and giving her too much freedom within my home. I believed, as an only child, she was enjoying being accepted and loved by my family. She was also a great help with Alistair, but as soon as we solved one problem, she presented us with another.

A QUEST FOR REVENGE

I realise in hindsight, I had not empowered her to make her own decisions. I discovered much later I had also created 'jealousy' between her mum and I. My foolishness caused me much heartache as her parents would bad mouth me to whoever they could find in our fellowship. Interestingly, none of those words stuck, even though this went on for over two years.

I learnt about forgiveness and discovered that it was easier to forgive a one-off offence, than one repeated regularly. Especially when people relayed to you what was being said behind your back. The Holy Spirit kept telling me, "I will vindicate you, forgive them."

At first, I forgave, and then I thought, "This is not working! What's the point, when they are still doing it?" I was getting angry and resentful. Patiently, I would hear the Holy Spirit say, "Forgive and bless them."

I replied, *"Bless them? Don't you know what they are saying about me?"*

"Bless them, my child."

Still thinking, "What do I bless them with? Should I bless them with rocks descending from you?"

"Bless them with everything you would like me to do for you."

An Open Door For 'Annabel'

I had no choice but to start praying that they would prosper in every godly endeavour; be good parents, full of God's love for one another. Each day I would bless them, and I gradually noticed how I sincerely desired with all my heart, to see them blessed. Their words and actions stopped affecting me; they bounced off.

Until the day I was standing behind someone who happened to be visiting our fellowship and saw my accuser pointing at me saying foul and unrepeatable things. I was more annoyed; they were giving a new visitor a bad impression of our church than what they said about me. I thought, "This must stop! I have had enough!" I went to see my elder the next day, who had initially been reluctant to get involved but on hearing of the recent instance, agreed with me.

I went home, pleased and satisfied that at last something would happen. I sat down with a cup of tea and thanked Father God that at last, the abuse would stop. Thinking he would say, 'Yes my child, I agree. You have been patient. Now it is time for this to stop,' what he said was so different!

"Does it matter?" was what I heard. I suddenly knew the truth. It did not matter what people thought about me. After all, they persecuted Jesus, spat at and reviled him. His hair was pulled out, he was whipped, he hung on the cross for me – yet there I was being angry and resentful about 'words'! I cried and saw my actions for what they were - acting out my anger, pride, resentment, and bitterness. I confessed my sins, repented and asked for forgiveness. When I phoned my elder and shared this with him, I could hear the relief in his voice. Now my heart was different, I carried on blessing them every day.

A few weeks later whilst out shopping, I spotted them heading towards me. I quickly hid behind a pillar, believing they would be unpleasant toward me. Praying the security camera would not notice me. I entered the next shop, only to see them again. This happened in four different shops, by now wondering if the Holy Spirit is setting me up. Or are they following me? In the fourth shop, before I could hide, they saw me and called me over.

I was surprised; they seem pleased to see me. They even asked after Alistair, Richard and my husband. They went on to tell me they were praying for Alistair's healing every day. I said goodbye, now completely confused by this interaction.

IN HIS TIME...

The following Sunday, the elder at the end of the service, requested anyone who required prayer to come to the front, so the ministry team could pray for them. Many responded, including *Annabel*'s mum, whom I decided to bypass but thought this would be impolite. I inquired if she would prefer someone else, but she quickly replied, "No, I wish to talk to you and apologise."

We both sat down so I could listen to her. "I need to repent of the things I have said and thought about you. Will you forgive me?" I was about to say *'yes'* when in a flash, the Holy Spirit showed me how threatened this woman had felt that her daughter spent more time with us than with them: making them believe she had loved *us* more than *them*. As the Holy Spirit revealed her anguish and fears, compassion and love for her filled my heart. Seeing her through Jesus' eyes I said, "Please forgive me for causing you so much pain and sorrow." We hugged and forgave each other: both crying. We became friends after this, and I encouraged *Annabel* to be less dependent on us and to spend quality time with her parents. When *Annabel* eventually left home, she chose to become a missionary and is now a powerful woman of God.

ENLARGING OUR HEARTS

Richard caught onto our love of people and he would befriend those whom others would normally find hard to be friends with. He became good friends with some gipsy children and would visit them in their caravans. It was not until many years later, I heard he used to be met by a man with a shotgun before they allowed him to enter the site.

Richard's big heart nearly got him into trouble. I noticed during meals; he would hide food in a napkin. Then food would disappear from the fridge. I was quiet about these new trends as I thought he was hungry, but when blankets disappeared, I tackled him.

He told me he had met a young lad who was squatting in a house down the road and he was taking food and blankets to him. He said "Mum, he has nothing. His mum has thrown him out!"

We agreed he would take me to meet this boy. I met the boy much quicker than I had imagined. I received a distressing phone call from Richard asking me to come to his school gates immediately as 'the boy' was bleeding badly, due to a wound from jagged glass and it was now soaking up everything they put on his wounds. After assessing the situation and looking at the injury, wound, I decided it was not as bad as they made out and brought him to our home.

As we entered our home, the gospel music I had on earlier, was still playing. He said, "I like that, what is it?" I told him it was Christian music about God's love. He sighed in pain as he lifted his shirt, showing me his scarred back; explaining his mum had whipped him after accusing him of stealing. He said their relationship had not been the same, since then and she had thrown him out of his home.

I recalled my home-help had told me about an unforgivable thing she had done by whipping her son for fear of him turning out like his imprisoned father. In responding, I had told her the good news of God's forgiveness, but she firmly believed her sin was unforgivable. After listening to the boy, I asked him where he lived and his mum's name. My home-help was his mother - what a coincidence it was!

I relayed about his mum sharing with me how she regretted beating him. He agreed she repeatedly said sorry, but every time she looked at him, she was reminded of his dad; whom she hates. As he was nearing eighteen, she could stand it no longer, so she threw him out to fend for himself.

When my husband came home, we discussed this young lad's dilemma and agreed the best course of action was for him to hand himself into the police before he got arrested. My husband went with him and unexpectedly, he was asked to stay while they questioned him. They told the young lad it worked to his favour that he had handed himself in. He would be taken to a youth offenders unit, as they had nowhere else to send him. Hearing this, my husband stepped in and said he could stay with us until after the trial. The police agreed on the condition that he acted as a guarantor. They were surprisingly relieved and told the young lad that going home with John, were a much better option than staying at the young offender's unit, until the trial. They sternly warned him: my husband only had to *'say the word'* if he misbehaved.

The young lad fitted into our family beautifully and became like another son. Gradually we noticed with affirmation, he started to believe in himself. The new clothes we bought him boosted his self-esteem. He would go out during the day to meet his friends and come home for meals. On his 18th birthday, we had a family party, and he felt overwhelmed by the goodwill and grateful for the birthday presents: he could hardly believe they were all for him. By this time, he had given his life to the Lord and attended church with us.

The forced-entry trial loomed over him, but the officer in charge of his case took a shine to him. He stated in his report, that our lad had inflicted the least amount of damage whilst breaking in. He had damaged nothing within the house and had left it spotless. Breaking and entry was a custodial offence, they had informed him. The officer said a character reference might be useful for judging his pending sentence. We gave a character reference while my church prayed. The people whose house he had broken into, also requested leniency on his behalf, if the window was replaced. My husband attended the trial and by God's grace, he only got a community sentence of sixteen hours and had to pay for the window. Once the trial now over, we sighed with relief! My church felt the Jesus Army would best meet his long-term needs, which he agreed to.

Many years later, we received a phone call from that same police officer who had remembered our kindness to the young lad. He requested if we could take in a young homeless girl. "Not a prostitute" he had said. "I think she is train-surfing. She has just experienced 'shock' after a man exposed himself to her." The officer did not want to leave her by herself. The only other option was a cell for the night, but she was only just 18 years old. Surprised at this request, I replied, "I would have to check with my husband." John said 'yes' instantly.

He went to fetch her from the police station. Later that day as she told us her story, my heart went out to her. She had lost her mum when she was young and was brought up by her dad who loved her, but all changed when he met another woman. Her stepmother hated her and was cruel to her. She finally made her dad choose between her and his daughter. Then, with tears soaking her dress, she pledged never to forgive her dad after pleading with him to allow her to stay as she had nowhere to go. But he had ignored her. Her stepmother told her to leave and never come back, instructing her to pack her bags, immediately.

She told us she had been train-surfing - a word which neither of us had heard of before. She often got no sleep, other than when someone watched over her and then she did the same for them. It sounded horrendous. With a roof over her head and having an address, she soon got a job; feeling quite proud of herself.

Gradually with prayer, the wounds of the rejections healed, and she loved going to church. She blossomed as a young lady and we all liked her. She became the daughter I never had. Unfortunately, my son became jealous and one day whilst we were out for the evening, I later found out, he had told her to leave. She had left before we got back. He had obviously not understood the impact of his actions.

Many months later, she turned up on our doorstep and told me the only way she had learnt to survive was to steal credit cards. She had come back to see me with this intention but could not do it after I told her how much we had missed and loved her. She dropped the credit card on the doormat as she left. I often wonder what happened to her.

I don't know if it was out of regret for making the girl leave our home as he had done, but from then onwards, and over the years, his bedroom was always available to people who needed a bed for the night: all young lads. When he went to college and started going to parties, his friends would stay the night, rather than go to their homes. I often offered them breakfast, but none were bothered about eating - it was more about the company and spending time together.

One youngster I remember was released from 'youth offenders unit' for shoplifting. Without an address, he was finding it hard to get a job. Using our address enabled him to find a job and eventually somewhere to stay. Young lads kicked out by their parents only needed to stay a few nights at ours and then went back home. They were of no bother to us, and company for Richard.

MORE KNOCKS ON OUR DOOR

People who needed help, prayer or deliverance seemed to find their way to our house. Many came from my church, but the visits became so frequent that we formed a team at the church to meet their demands. Word soon went around that we would pray for people's inner healing and deliverance if needed. There were five of us to start with and before long the team became larger. I decided we all needed training and devised a training programme by watching and listening to videos by Bill Subritzky on deliverance; we listened to Derek Prince Cassettes on *The Blood* and other relevant teachings. All team members read *Emotionally Free* by Rita Bennett. We would then eat together, get to know each other and practise on one another, what we had learnt. I noticed that prior to this training, we had not asked people about their background, so we devised a new, more in-depth questionnaire asking about past traumas and history before their appointments. All our training showed dividends, as we witnessed a rapid change in the people we ministered to. I was now officially appointed as the leader of the ministering team.

One time, after a visiting speaker shared about his abuse, we were inundated with people needing ministration and it caused us to use every available room in the church. Soon, I had five teams and each team comprised at least four people. Two would take it in turns to minister, the other two would quietly pray in the background, after which we switched roles. I would be called in as the trouble-shooter when I was not ministering to people.

We learnt by trial and error. At first, we were ministering to people all day, until we set guidelines as we were getting tired. We would start at ten o'clock, pray and worship as a team and then minister until 1 pm. Sometimes, a person could need ministering until 3 pm, close to home-time for the children. We took a break during the school holidays. As we became more experienced, what had taken us hours now took less time. The elders were so impressed with the results, they advised the whole leadership team to go for ministry.

London churches heard and sent their difficult cases, especially those who had been witches. They needed a specialist form of deliverance, but God was faithful, as He taught us on the job and they stayed free.

I remember one time; the Holy Spirit led us to ask them to renounce their occult name. The first time I relayed this, the person was most surprised and found this hard to do. We later found out when people are initiated into witchcraft they are given an occult name and demons are assigned to help them. We also established not to carry on if those who claimed to be serious about freedom were not willing to renounce their names. We read books by people who had a ministry in this field. Rebecca Brown's, *Prepare for War* and *Vessel of Honour* helped us and what we did not know, the Holy Spirit taught us. We witnessed people completely set free without us praying for them.

One former witch came to see me and said, "I used to be a witch and I need deliverance." As she spoke, I heard the Holy Spirit say, "I do not want you to pray for her." I thought, "She is asking for help and seems genuine. Why not? Is she a plant or a *set-up*? Am I hearing correctly? Maybe this is deception and not the Holy Spirit" These thoughts whizzed through my mind, so I asked her, for more time, to pray for direction from God. Again, the Holy Spirit said, "I do not want you to pray for her." I carried on seeking direction, but I still heard the same instruction not to pray for her. Then, the Holy Spirit said, "Ask her to get baptised." I went back to her with this and added that I believed as she got baptised, God will deliver her. Somewhat surprised by this instruction, she agreed to Baptism and came up, out of the baptismal water-free! Never again to be harassed by demons.

GOSSIP A DESTINY BLOCKER

I nearly mucked up my destiny, but in Father God's kindness, He sent Jesus. One of the leader's wives shared a word with me in confidence and told me not to tell anyone. Normally, I jealously guarded people's confidences, but this particular time, I did not view what she had told me as important, so I shared what she had told me with a friend. *Sometimes, we are not aware of the implications of our actions*, and what happened next made me aware of this. I was sitting in my front room reading my bible when Jesus appeared in my room. He did not look too pleased and his tone when he rebuked me evoked the fear of God in me. I instantly knew what he was talking about and how he viewed what I had done. I was now lying flat on the floor, wondering if I would live. Is this what the fear of God is like? Then Jesus' tone changed to a kind, loving voice, so much so, I tentatively raised my head to look up; *thankful that I will live*. "Gossip cannot be part of your life otherwise it will affect your destiny" Smiling at me as he said this. I repented, and he disappeared as fast as he had arrived.

Knowing I had no time to lose, I phoned the leader's wife and repented of what I had done. She was surprised and angry I had told someone. She asked for the name of the person. She said, "I will phone and tell them not to listen to gossip." I requested a time to phone and repent for what I had done. After this, she became fierce about stamping out gossip in our fellowship, especially amongst the women. If I was being engaged in gossip, I learnt to free myself and would politely say, "I would rather not listen to this. Please excuse me."

Have you ever gossiped? Most of us have some point in our life.

Why not repent and ask the Holy Spirit to show you anything seeking to block God's plan and destiny for you?

CHAPTER 9

ANGELS

Angels

Hebrews 1:14

Are they not all ministering spirits, sent forth to minister for them who shall be heirs of salvation?

The ministry of angels is real. Angels are mentioned more in the New Testament than they are in the Old Testament. Every believer has at least two angels

Mathew 18:10 (KJV)

Take heed that ye despise not one of these little ones; for I say unto you, That in heaven their angels do always behold the face of my Father which is in heaven.

Angels which essentially means 'messengers' have many functions. They share information (Luke 1:5-25, 26-38 and John 20). In Luke I:5-25 he appeared to Zacharias whose wife Elizabeth was barren.

And there appeared unto him an angel of the Lord standing on the right side of the altar of incense. And when Zacharias saw him, he was troubled, and fear fell upon him. But the angel said unto him, Fear not, Zacharias: for thy prayer is heard; and thy wife Elisabeth shall bear thee a son, and thou shalt call his name John.

Zacharias did not believe him and verse 19 says where he came from and his function.

And the angel answering said unto him, I am Gabriel, that stands in the presence of God, and am sent to speak unto thee, and to shew thee these glad tidings.

Angels offer protection Psalm 91:11
For he shall give his angels charge over thee, to keep thee in all thy ways.

Angels deliver provision as they did to Elijah when he had fled from Jezebel (1King 19:5) *And as he lay and slept under a juniper tree, behold, then an angel touched him, and said unto him, Arise and eat.*

Angels War on your behalf *(2 Kings 19:34-35)*
For I will defend this city, to save it, for mine own sake, and for my servant David's sake. And it came to pass that night that the angel of the Lord went out, and smote in the camp of the Assyrians a hundred fourscore and five thousand: and when they arose early in the morning, behold, they were all dead corpses.

Angels obey the word of God as borne out in Psalm 103:20
Bless the Lord, ye his angels that excel in strength, that do his commandments, hearkening unto the voice of his word.
All my experiences of angels have been different. When Alistair was about 2 years old, a friend asked me to give her a lift to the hospital to visit her son: recently diagnosed with meningitis. On our way back, it started to rain so heavily, we couldn't see in front of us. Apprehensively driving down a very steep hill which joined a three-way junction, which in normal weather I would approach with great caution, but now I couldn't even see if cars were coming.

There was no way of turning around as the hill was so steep, I had no other choice than to try and cross it.

Did I pray? I am not sure. Suddenly, out of nowhere a figure of a large man dressed in bright-yellow marine waterproofs with a matching yellow boat-shaped hat, stood in the middle of the road as if he had every right to be there. I could see him clearly, even though a second ago, I could not see in front of me. The sight of him was reassuring. He walked in front of the car as I crawled to the junction, still not knowing if there was oncoming traffic. I stopped unsure of what to do, and then he waved me on to cross the junction as if he knew it was clear. I did not hesitate but crossed the road.

As I drove on, I started to laugh; partly as the figure in the boat-shaped hat reminded me of a children's cartoon character but also realised I was overflowing with joy. I burst into spontaneous worship at which the sun came out. I looked back in the mirror but could see no sign of the man. I slowed the car down, rerunning what had just happened in my mind and came to the conclusion; there was nowhere for him to have appeared from. Or maybe there was a side road I was unaware of.

Strange, I wondered. *Was that an angel? But he was not dressed in white, but I didn't see any wings and why do I feel so happy?*

In an earlier chapter, I captured my experience of dying and going to heaven. The angel that came for me was what I call *the traditionally dressed angel* - long white robe, *he* did not speak verbally to me, but I knew in my spirit what he was saying.

The next time was so different and again unexpected. Alistair was seven years old and a young girl who used to babysit for us said she felt that Alistair should go to a special evening meeting at our church with a visiting-speaker Ron Simms. I knew this man use to be a gangster and God had set him free, changing his life and he now had a healing ministry. At first, I said no as it was past Alistair's bedtime, but she phoned again and said she felt we should go.

I talked it over with my husband who agreed he would babysit my other son. The meeting was good, but my blood ran cold when Alistair in the middle of the service let out a blood curling scream. We were asked to go forward and Ron prayed for Alistair with another man called John Smith, and then they prayed for me. I felt cared for and ministered to but saw no visible change in Alistair.

A week later, I was informed by someone at my church, John Smith whilst driving home from the meeting, had been so overcome with emotion, he had to pull over and then the Holy Spirit spoke to him about Alistair. You can imagine my curiosity to know what the Holy Spirit had said to him.

It took over a week for her to give me his telephone number. My husband John was away for the night on business. *What an ideal time!* I thought to phone John Smith but first I needed to share my heart with God.

> *Father God, I am confused. I believe that you have told me that Alistair is going to be healed; Ernie a man I greatly respect has said to me I believe that Alistair's healing is going to be in heaven not on earth. Yet I believe this will happen on earth. Will you tell me if I am wrong?*

I then decided to phone John Smith. By then tucked up in bed with the phone on my lap, started to dial his number when I experienced the fright of my life. A man dressed in a black suit was standing at the end of my bed. The suddenness of this had me pressed right against the bed head. If I could have run, I would have. He said, "Do not fear, I am a messenger sent by God. What you are about to hear is a word from God to you." I looked at the man he had long blonde hair, shoulder-length, big blue eyes, a kind, tanned face. As I looked at his suit I thought, *"God couldn't you do better!"* His suit looked so old fashioned. As I looked at the suit I could see through it to a gold sash around his waist. The bed blocked what he was wearing on his feet.

Somehow, my fear abated still looking at him: phone in my hand. John Smith answered, and I told him who I was and that there was an angel standing at the bottom of my bed. He seemed to either not hear or choose to ignore this and started to tell me what happened when he started to cry. John said he could not stop praying as he drove home on the motorway, filled with compassion for Alistair. Awash with tears he had to pull over as he couldn't see where he was going. As he did, the Holy Spirit started to reveal how to pray as there had been *bestiality* four-generations back, in my family line.

As he finished telling me this, he started to prophesy. I was amazed at what he was saying and listened intently; my mind wandering when he mentioned "My thoughts are not your thoughts, neither are your ways my ways" *Not again! I thought.* I was fed up of hearing this verse, but I perked up when he carried on. At the end of the call, he said, "I don't normally prophesy." I looked up and realised the angel had gone. Normally when John my husband was away I slept fretfully hearing every noise. What a difference! From then on, I slept soundly. The angel had left a beautiful, tangible peace in the atmosphere. Not just in our bedroom but in the whole house. People comment on it even now.

The next morning, I awoke, and my first thought was: *Did I imagine what happened last night? Oh no, I did not write down what John Smith had said.* As I thought about this I could see words written across my forehead, almost as if my mind was a blackboard. As I wrote each line down they vanished.

Angels

This is what I wrote down:
> You are called to war
>
> Make a straight path
>
> I have prepared the way
>
> I will show you the way to go
>
> For my thoughts are not your thoughts
>
> Not your ways, but my ways, says the Lord
>
> I have appointed the man,
>
> the place and the time
>
> To bring glory to my son
>
> I will heal your son,
>
> This will bring great glory to my name
>
> and hundreds of thousands will come
>
> to know me through this.

Soon after this happened, I shared this with one of the elders' wives who said she didn't believe me. My thoughts were; *if she does not believe me, what will others think?* So I told no one until many years later when asked to testify what God was doing in my life. I found myself sharing about the angel and the prophecy. Not a pin-drop could be heard from the audience. By their response knew they believed me and they wanted *to go to war* (meaning spiritual warfare) there and then. This resulted in praying for Alistair for a few weeks but when they did not see any change, people lost heart and stopped.

An interesting fact about the angel's attire was that I saw the exact same suit on a dummy in Burtons (a men's retail shop) a few weeks later and I jokingly wondered if the angel had borrowed this from them. I heard of another testimony from The Ron Simms meeting which had been videoed. A man had written in to say he had given his life to the lord after hearing Alistair's scream, as he suddenly became convicted that he needed to repent as hell was real.

Years later Alistair had to have an operation on his legs. After the operation, he came around but then went into a comma. While in a clinical comma he would laugh the most beautiful laugh I have ever heard, which somehow reassured us he would be alright as he seemed to be enjoying himself. I had not yet shared this with anyone in church when the youth group (shared with me that while praying) they saw Alistair playing with angels. Other people came up to me and confirmed this.

The way Alistair came out of that comma was also supernatural. When my elder asked me how Alistair was doing, I told him he was still in the comma but what he heard me say was that *Alistair had come out of the comma. With* excitement, he went ahead to share the 'testimony' with the church, and they all started clapping, rejoicing and thanking God. I stood there in a quandary not knowing what to do. Should I correct him? I wondered.

Angels

I couldn't stay for the whole service as I had to relieve John at the hospital. On my way, I pondered on how to tell my elder he had misheard me. To my greatest relief and joy, when I got there lo and behold: Alistair was out of the comma sitting up, sipping a drink. It turned out that at the time we were clapping, rejoicing and thanking God, Alistair came out of the comma. This is another example of the power of thanksgiving.

Many years later, at the same church, I started sharing with a stranger about the angel appearing not having thought about it since the church had stopped praying. I mentioned how amazed I was that I was sharing the experience and he said, looking into my eyes, "it's time to share." I was astonished by his words and was about to give him a reply when he again said, "It's time to share," then he disappeared. I looked around for him and spoke to others to find out if had they too had seen him, but no one had.

Soon after 'the messenger's' coming and the prophecy given for Alistair, I had another experience of an angel. This time I was praying with a friend and we were both asking God what our calling was. This angel appeared to both of us: nearer to my friend than me, but only spoke to me and said, "You are like a bull in a china shop, but you will not always be this way. You are called to bring healing to the captives and set the captives free." Then he recited Isaiah 61 over me. Then emphasized, "The whole of Isaiah 61 is your calling which you are being equipped to do."

He disappeared as fast as he had come. My friend said afterwards, that she could not see him fully but could see his shape and felt his presence. Both so stunned, we hardly said a word to each other. She did not hear him speak. I was grateful she had been their otherwise I would not have believed what happened.

Another completely different experience of angels happened during a deliverance ministry. We had a policy, after praying a while for a person; we would stop to put our focus back on our heavenly Father (rather than on the devil) and would worship God. This time we started to worship and the only way to describe it was our voices were drowned out by the sound of what seemed like a choir, which completely filled the room. It was like nothing I had ever heard before - beautiful, and our own voices sounded wonderful as well. We were all flat on our faces, knowing we were experiencing something sacred. This went on for about ten minutes. The deliverance took a few minutes after that.

It did not stop there… As we walked into our elder's office eager to tell him what had just happened. We were met by the most enormous angel I have ever seen! His head was above the rooftop and yet we could see all of him. He wore normal clothes, stood between us and our elder's desk, which he was sitting behind. In our spirits we received a 'well done' then he vanished. He gave the impression of strength and I wondered if he was an angel sent to watch and protect the team as we prayed for people. Our elder could not see the angel but we could. We were so stunned. We all left quietly. Checking with each other when we got home did you see what I saw?

Every time I have shared my angel stories and others share theirs' it seems to stir up heavenly activity and we have often ended up praying for people and seeing people healed or a miraculous provision. One time as a lady walked past us. She froze and ended up sitting and chatting with us. She ended up giving her life to the Lord.

After a time of sharing our angel stories, my inquisitive friends asked, "Have you seen their wings?" I replied no, and I also wonder what they are like.

I am sure they were listening because a few days later we were on a mission trip in Cumbria, ministering to the church's leadership team. I was praying for one of the ladies when I looked behind her and saw a large angel's wing. To my surprise, it was not all white. It looked as if it had tinges of pink and the feathers looked soft. The feathers were laid out a bit like a swan's wing: elegant very beautiful but also powerful. I watched as the wings outstretched and they seemed to be making the smallest movement almost a quiver. At the same time, the lady in question said she felt strange and all in a quiver she fell on the floor.

I moved onto the next person and started to pray; again, I saw an angel's wings behind them. Not seeing the angel just, the wings, I had the impression I was not seeing them fully outstretched. As the angel fluttered his wings the person I was praying for fell to the floor. When I spoke to both people afterwards, they felt different. The whole room seemed to be filled with joy and we started to laugh.

I sat down on a beanbag, pondering on what had just happened; I started to pray and thank God. The next thing I knew, I was asleep and woke up totally refreshed. To this day, I still think the angels were showing off and saying to me, "Look, we do have wings!" As well as ministering to the people I felt privileged to have seen their wings up close.

I have seen Angels many times, sometimes in church services and other times in my mind's eye. One funny instance which could have turned out so differently was when my eldest son, Richard, used to have a cross country motorbike. This day, he was in our village, riding behind a car. He said the car stopped suddenly, causing him to hit the back of the car. The driver said he saw him fly over his bonnet and hit the road with a thud. He was very shaken and believed Richard was seriously injured if not dead.

By the time I got there, Richard was standing, arguing with the ambulance men, refusing to go to the hospital but when the driver told them what had happened, they advised him to go. The doctors at the Accident and Emergency were amazed as he had no bruises on him or any form of injury. They made him retell what had happened several times, but not believing him.

The driver phoned later and could not believe he was uninjured. The driver did not claim against Richard and just kept saying, "I believed he was dead." I said Jesus was looking after him; he said, "I thought I had killed him."

When I prayed to God about it, with thanksgiving, the Holy Spirit showed me this argument going on in heaven with Richards angels. God had called for a reinforcement of angels and the angels kept saying it is such hard work, keeping him safe. Which, I could understand, as Richard loved to do stunts with his motorbike. He also did very frightening double-somersault manoeuvres on his snowboard: later in life becoming a stunt rider for a stunt team.

Then I saw a movie picture of the accident playing out in front of me. Angels were holding onto his hair, legs and arms as he flew through the air and hit the road. One angel supported his head, another under him as he landed. I did laugh. Or maybe I imagined it. All I know is that he did not have a scratch or bruise on him after hitting the back of the car with a force that flung him over the car and landing on the road. The front wheel of his motorbike was completely buckled from the impact and had to be replaced.

I personally have found it reassuring that we have angels watching over us. As I have pressed in for more of the *seer gift*, I often see them as I minister to people and sometimes the demons as well. I do not see them all the time. Sometimes I just sense their presence, or the Holy Spirit will show me what they are doing.

I have observed that if I watch anything violent or disturbing on the television, I do not see or sense them for months and they do not return until I repent and ask the Holy Spirit to cleanse me and specifically, my *eye gate*.

DISAPPOINTMENT

This becomes a familiar feature of life, for parents and caregivers of disabled children. While there are many books on prayer and other popular topics, few books address how to handle disappointments and loss. When my son was diagnosed with cerebral palsy (brain damage) at an early age and spastic quadriplegia, affecting all four limbs, I had limited books to help me through my disappointment. Years later, I was told he was totally blind with 40% hearing loss in one ear and 80% in the other. I felt like a pinball machine, being aimed at by this hard metal ball: hitting me wherever it could: gut-wrenching. *'Loss'* almost became a continuous part of my life. At six weeks old, I was overjoyed when Alistair first smiled now seven weeks old Alistair was not smiling spontaneously as he saw our faces. In this season of disappointments and loss, we also saw amazing miracles happen. After being told by Great Ormond Street, Alistair had a rare eye condition (a severed optic nerve in his eye which caused complete blindness: most blind people can see something) I found this news more devastating than being told he had brain damage. It seemed cruel, on top of all, he had to contend with. I fell apart, so much so, that I was sent a counsellor to talk to me. Bless her. She was not much help or maybe the timing was too soon for me to listen to her or anyone else.

I would lie in the bath with eyes tightly closed, imagining what it must be like not being able to see. I would then try to get out of the bath without opening my eyes. Although I had the advantage of memory, I still bashed into the towel rail. Sometimes I would drop the towel and then have to feel for it. I cried and cried, telling God that he needed to heal Alistair as this was too much. I pleaded with God; he would not be totally blind. It seemed very unfair on Alistair and I remember thinking, "Is this the result of my involvement in witchcraft?"

I waited outside the ophthalmic consultant's room for over half an hour without Alistair. After examining him, the consultant said he needed to perform some tests. As time passed, I wondered what is going on as I had still not been called back in. When he finally did, he said, "A miracle has occurred! Your son's optic nerve has re-joined and there is life in it now. The last time I examined him, his optic nerve was dead. I needed other opinions; they also confirmed a 'working optic nerve'. We have all concurred that this is a miracle. It means that according to what's happening in his brain, he will see shadows and sometimes his sight will be better than other days. He is no longer completely blind but will still be on the blind register." I was hardly able to stay still in the chair, as he told me about Alistair's miracle. Joy flooded me; I wanted to jump up and hug him. I said, "God loves to do miracles." This miracle manifested as we went home with Alistair laughing at the shadows, the trees cast as we passed them in the car.

Years later, Alistair was six by then, after many tests on Alistair's hearing, the consultant told me he had significant hearing loss. We had wondered about his hearing, but it seemed to fluctuate. I was familiar with the reality of what this would be like for Alistair as I had also been deaf at age four with no one picking up on it. I had mastered lip-reading. I knew with Alistair's sight problems, this was not an option, for him. Now, Alistair, they were saying a hearing aid might help. He pulled out the hearing aid and no matter what we tried, he refused to tolerate it. I spent one whole day just praying for this one miracle - for God to restore his hearing.

After turning down the consultants' advice on an operation to insert grommets, I insisted that Alistair, who was now twelve, responds to what we said and seems to understand us. The consultant made it clear, he did not believe us. With the level of

Alistair's hearing loss, he should not normally be capable of hearing without a hearing aid. He said there was now a way to prove this by connecting him to a new special machine. This would also enable them to find out what type of hearing loss he had. The drawback was it would need to be done under aesthetic and with Alistair's epilepsy this placed him at risk. After discussion with parties involved, it was decided the risks were slight.

Having run tests on Alistair over the years, he could not believe the test results. The tests showed normal hearing other than there would be fluctuations when he had a cold.

God knows what we can bear, and the following promise has been a comfort over the years as *a bruised reed he will not break*. Losing not being able to share milestones with others, often happening years later, Alistair crawled when eight years old, we were so excited at this. The first time he rolled over on his own, he was aged about two years old and understandably, his achievements did not have the same impact on others as they did on us. We felt alone in our celebrations.

I used to hold evening parties, selling children's clothes when Alistair was about three. This gave me a break from Alistair's needs and enabled me to meet other mums. I listened politely, but heartbroken as they talked about what their children were doing. Some were the same age as Alistair, but I would avoid saying I had a disabled child at all cost as it was an anecdote to killing the party spirit.

In my experience, the grief would sneak up at the oddest times. One day, I was busy cheering Richard at his school's Sports Day, when suddenly I found myself fighting back tears at the realisation Alistair may never run a race.

Life was unusual for Richard too. He was growing up with a disabled brother: unable to play football with or catch a ball. He even tried to teach Alistair to catch a ball with a bell in it. We would play football using the wheelchair to boot the ball. But times when Richard voiced from his heart, "*I wish Alistair could play with me properly,*" my heart would break for him.

The day Alistair said 'dad' then later 'mum', we counted thirteen words he could now use appropriately. The school did not believe us, and before we could prove it, Alistair had a grand mal seizure, ending up in the hospital for two weeks. Each time he had a severe seizure it wiped out any previous learning. No matter how hard we tried, he did not seem to regain whatever he had lost. The same happened with crawling. He had not established enough knowledge about crawling in his memory bank, so he lost the ability to crawl after another grand mal episode, resulting in an even longer stay at the hospital because they could not stabilize him. At first, not realising what had happened, we expected him to crawl and talk again. Before we could compute one loss, we were onto the next crisis.

Some disappointments were of my doing. Or so I believed. I would join all the dots together and conclude on the right time for Alistair's healing. One of those times was at the 'Cross Roads 2000' event which took place in 1998. Evangelist Reinhard Bonnke who is principally known for his 'Great Gospel Crusades' throughout Africa was to be the main speaker at the conference. His reputation for the healings that happened at his crusades, with people getting out of wheelchairs and walking, excited us. The churches had erected an enormous marquee: my church was involved with the counselling for salvation and intercession. They had asked my husband to help with the running and erection of the video walls - normally used by him abroad and at the Royal Tournaments.

This must be it! I thought, looking at the wording of the prophecy given for Alistair, "I have appointed, the man, the time, the place to bring glory to my son, I will heal your son."

Thinking, *"Surely God you would want my husband there when it happens. The day would be Saturday when most people attend as Father God would want it witnessed by as many people as possible. How clever of God to bring this man all the way from Africa and my husband would be there - perfect in every way!"*

The wheelchairs all lined up in the front row and I remember thinking, "What a lot of wheelchairs!" I noticed several children similar to Alistair there and many adults too. A lady came up and prayed for Alistair. Later I found out her name was Jean Darnell. She shared with me, a picture she saw: not understanding it. She saw a fish swimming round and round in a fishbowl. "Do ask God what it means," she said. I wondered if she had heard correctly, not knowing she was a famous, respected Christian leader.

Reinhard Bonkee announced he would pray for all those in wheelchairs before the start of the meeting. The excitement in the air as his entourage followed him was palatable. He came towards me; I took Alistair's safety harness off leaving nothing to hinder him from getting up and walking. He prayed for Alistair putting his hand on his head; Alistair slumped forward, slithering onto the floor. "Should I get him up onto his feet?" I asked myself desperate for something to happen – hoping to see him walk." At the same time not wanting to impede what the Holy Spirit was doing; I was in a real quandary also knowing the ground was damp. Alistair started to protest, and someone helped me get him back in his wheelchair.

With Alistair back in his wheelchair, I looked over to see what was happening. Reinhard Bonkee was now praying for people about ten wheelchairs away. Suddenly, he stopped in his tracks looked back towards me and then I realised he was coming back. It was so funny his entourage did not know what to do; he passed through the middle of them and headed back. Standing in front of me, he made eye contact and said "God says to you, don't give up, keep on asking. Remember, He said, don't give up - keep on asking," Then he disappeared back to praying for the others: his entourage having caught up with him by then.

Amazed and surprised at what had just happened, I put Alistair's safety harness back on him, looking and seeing no change. I felt a wave of disappointment creep up all over me, starting with a torturing thought.

I now know how to take these thoughts captive and make them obedient to God. Back then, I would feel it reach my heart with unbearable pain. I felt my heart shutting down, unable to deal with the emotions. I would numb myself in order to deal with the disappointment. Some leaders I knew prayed for Alistair and one of them said, "if only we could find one righteous man."

Stirring up hope and thinking, "There is still time, he hasn't preached yet, often healings happened whilst he preaches." When he announced that Suzette Hatti would be preaching, I was disappointed. It was her first time of speaking and he had just sprung it on her. She was so anointed; it riveted me hearing her preach on Prayer and Alistair seemed to enjoy it – as he was quiet the whole time. All through the sermon, I watched Alistair closely, for the slightest change. The meeting ended with many salvations but few healings. People were saying it was *'the witches who had stopped the healings'*, but my mind screamed at them, "Don't you realise *Greater is he in you than he who is in the world!*" Part of me kept wondering was this so. Yet I chose to agree it was rubbish: what they are saying. All these thoughts were going through my mind. My mind had a *field day*. As I turned to go home, the Holy Spirit spoke into my mind so vividly, as if on a screen.

For as the rains come down, and the snow from heaven,
And do not return there,
But water the earth,
And make it bring forth and bud,
That it may give seed to the sower
And bread to the eater,
[11] So shall My word be that goes forth from My mouth;
It shall not return to Me void,
But it shall accomplish what I please,
And it shall prosper in the thing for which I sent it.

As he imprinted this word in me, I knew it was from the book of Isaiah. I later discovered it was Isaiah 55. When I looked this up, I noticed the wording of Alistair's prophesy came just before this passage.

For My thoughts are not your thoughts, nor are your ways My
ways, says the Lord. For as the heavens are higher than the earth, so are

My ways higher than your ways,
And My thoughts than your thoughts.

Though bitterly disappointed, I took heart from this scripture and the promise it contained, understanding a little of what it meant when He said, "My thoughts are not your thoughts, nor are my ways your ways."

My husband told me he nearly gave his life to the Lord at the crusade but his duty to the video wall blocked him from responding when the call for salvation came.

You would think I learnt my lesson but over the years, I forgot what I had learnt. Again, I would tell God how he should do it. *"Just in case you do not realise Richard is growing up fast surely you would want him to play with his brother."* I would remind God. Another time, "Richard is getting married this would be a good time."

One big lesson I learnt was that the enemy loves to pile on guilt and condemnation: saying, *'you are not praying enough.'* Then when I did, *'you're not praying right', 'you should read your bible more'*. When the enemy was saying, "you should do this or that, I recognised who was behind the lie - the accuser of the brethren. He would pick up on things I had said to others, I wish I had more time to pray and read the bible. Satan cannot read your thoughts but has a book on your life written by what he sees and hears you say and will try to predict what might happen and is out to stop your reaching your destiny. The cool thing is he often gets it completely wrong and overplays his hand. *Scripture confirms that there is no guilt or condemnation for those who are in Christ Jesus.*

Father God one day, said, "You are praying from a place of entitlement," and led me to study about grace and faith.

When I prayed for the sick, the thought, "How can you pray for the sick when your own son is not healed." Satan was unaware I that had a dream in which I was being interviewed by a TV presenter who said, "You have a healing ministry and yet your own son is not healed. How can that be?" I heard myself reply well that just proves its God's power and not mine. I laughed at the audacity of this thought and relaxed, watching what God would do for those whose healing I prayed for.

People encouraged me to take Alistair to healing meetings, I only went to a few when he was young. After each time, I found handling the disappointment painful. I would pull myself together each time, thinking: *It will happen next time.* The Holy Spirit gently showed me my prayers were full of my *needs* and *wants*. I made a point from then on to pray more for others, than for my own needs and this was the start of my intercession prayer ministry. I held prayer meetings in my house; encouraged by answers to our prayers. Before we had finished asking, we witnessed our prayers being answered in extraordinary ways. Gradually the Holy Spirit taught me to trust him, whether I saw the manifestation of the healing or not and to worship him for who he is rather than for what he can do for me.

I was doing really well with my eyes fixed on Jesus, and his promises when one night the thought bombarded my mind: *does Jesus really heal?* I felt myself wobble; as the thought seemed so real. Part of me tried rejecting it, the other battling to prove it.

I prayed, then saw on the screen of my inner vision Jesus standing before me and I heard him say, *"Touch the hem of my garment"*. Again, Jesus repeated the same words. I had such an intense desire to touch the hem of his garment thinking I wonder if this is how the lady with the issue of blood felt. Believing as she touched the hem of his garment, Jesus would heal her. Father give me unshakable faith as I touch Jesus's hem no matter what I see in the natural I will believe you for Alistair's healing. Suddenly I envisaged myself as the women trying desperately, longingly to reach Jesus, crawling on the ground, trying to clutch his garment before he moved off. I clutched his hem, feeling it in my hand as I did, all doubt and unbelief left. The vision disappeared but I now felt an unshakable faith that Alistair would receive his healing and not look at what I am seeing, to keep on asking as instructed, but now praying from the place of victory. My faith now seeing it as done, standing and claiming the prophetic words over his life.

Not knowing then, I would need this unshakeable faith when Alistair did not come fully round after a second operation on his legs. The doctors said he was slipping into a coma and they needed to act fast. The glass phial in his hand shattered so the doctor asked for another, but the same thing happened again. All this while my husband and son saw what was going on. The word 'curse' came to mind and at that instance, someone asked us to leave. Knowing they had despatched the sister to run to another part of the hospital to get another phial so they could inject Alistair and bring him out of this comma. Richard was upset at what he had seen while I, did not care who was listening as I broke any curses, words, influences and obstacles that were seeking to harm Alistair and rob him of God's plan and destiny.

Alistair recovered before the expected six weeks after the operation. Within four weeks he was ready to go home with an additional four weeks in plaster. His swift recovery was remarked upon by his consultant, at his follow-up appointments.

When Alistair was about fifteen, they carried out a pioneering surgery on his legs as they were scissoring; causing difficulties when we changed him. This was a risky surgery as they would move every muscle and tendon: rerouting them. There was a danger Alistair's brain may not interpret the changes and he would have no movement in his legs. They also had never done this surgery on a child of Alistair's age. The surgery would take all day and they would need two orthopaedic surgeons one for each leg. If we agreed, he would find another consultant to join him. There was also a risk to Alistair, being under anaesthetic that long. We prayed, and God gave my husband and me an immense sense of peace. To cut a long story short, the operation was a complete success.

The nurse who was monitoring Alistair, after this operation, made an angry comment about my lack of worry. "Don't you know Alistair is still in danger?" Once she had calmed down and she questioned why I had been so peaceful. I shared this *'peace'* that came from Jesus, with her and told her she could have it too. She ended up asking Jesus into her life and I had most of the day to disciple her. After a month, Alistair, surprised everyone, by being able to stand, plastered to his hips with a broom handle parting his legs. We were in the hospital for two months and were allowed towards the end, to take him home for the weekend. The first weekend was a complete disaster; I found it backbreaking moving him, plastered to his hips and changing him, proved difficult - he had to return to the hospital. But the second attempt two weeks later was more successful. As for getting him in and out of the car, *I am sure* God provided angels to assist us as looking back, we are not sure how we did this. At the hospital, it took three of us getting him into the car safely, and God was always aware I would need help on the other end. Believing God would provide the help, sometimes it was by giving me superhuman strength and because Alistair was pleased to be home, he co-operated.

RISING FROM DISAPPOINTMENT

The following steps have been useful in picking myself up after a disappointment. I would love to hear from you if they help you, or maybe you have some of your own you would like to share with me.

Acknowledge the disappointment and all the emotions that come with it. Whether it is pain in the heart, overwhelming grief, hopelessness. It could even be *angry* at yourself for getting it wrong or anger at God (maybe) for feeling He *'let you down'*.

The Word says, "Hope deferred makes the heart sick."

Confess any doubt, unbelief, resentment ask for his forgiveness, knowing he has already forgiven you.

Let go of **Self-pity** and *choose* not to partner with it. I talk at length about how the Holy Spirit delivered me from self-pity in another part of the book.

Avoid **masking the pain.** Disappointment not dealt with turns to discouragement. We look at the circumstances and sometimes other people rather than the cause, our reactions and our feelings. I noticed the grief became less when I cried and cried, asking the Holy Spirit to use my tears as a healing balm.

Cry when you need to. Crying helps unleash the numbing which can sometimes happen to our emotions and feelings. I could numb myself by pretending the situation didn't matter; knowing this was not the truth. As we push down and bury our true feelings and emotions, the impact of the shock and trauma gets stored in our bodies causing unexplainable somatic pain. Pain needs to come out and be given to God. Otherwise, the anger-pain can turn to depression; waiting to be unravished later.

The Holy Spirit is our healer, and he loves to be given permission to do His job. The impact of the trauma and shock I had seen and experienced did not have its impact on me, until many years later.

Take care of yourself. When we don't want to face pain, we can overwork, overeat; we can invent ways to distract us from the real issue. If your body isn't working, your mind and emotions can become weaker. I love how God tended to Elijah's body first—before addressing anything else by providing the ravens to feed him. Sometimes the circumstances of life drain us dry, and we need to press pause, stop doing, rest and refresh. Give yourself permission to stop.

Establish a good healthy routine. Go to bed at a reasonable time Get up after eight to nine hours of sleep. Some of my clients have found that laughing even when if they have to fake it, helps and they end up belly laughing. Laugh at the lies.

I love the African culture of relatives and even strangers visiting people for over a week: wailing, crying - giving you permission to scream if need be when grief or a loss happens.

Choose to be Thankful. I go into depth about thanksgiving in another chapter. Changing my thinking and attitude to one of thankfulness was key to my healing. The power of thankfulness altered my perception of how I viewed obstacles and challenges. I would intentionally look for something to thank God for. I would start with thanking God for my salvation, my husband, two healthy and loving sons. Then I would ask the Holy Spirit to show me something in a drastic situation that I could thank him for, and he always did. By doing this, I was renewing my mind with truth, which brought my thoughts into alignment with God's word. Gratitude is a powerful anecdote for discouragement. We may find it hard to give God thanks for the difficult situation we find ourselves in, but we can learn to look for things we can be thankful for during it.

Train yourself to "see" life out of two lenses at the same time. When the apostle Paul refers to being transformed by the renewing of our mind, he is telling us that our minds need to be trained to think differently than we have in the past. Part of this training is to learn to see both the temporal (life is hard) and the eternal (God has a purpose here) at the same time.

Paul never minimized the pain of the temporal, yet discouragement didn't win because he knew that God's purposes were at work. He spoke honestly of his temporal pain when he said he was *"Hard-pressed on every side, perplexed, persecuted and struck down."* Yet he did not become crushed, despairing nor destroyed. Why not? Because he learnt to firmly fix his spiritual eyes on the eternal perspective. He says, "Therefore we do not lose heart... So *we fix our eyes not on what is seen, but on what is unseen.* For what is seen is *temporary*, but what is unseen is *eternal*" (2 Corinthians 4:8-18). These scriptures helped and continue to give me hope for the future.

Ask God for a 'Word' about your situation. I would ask God for a promise or *Word* I could hold on to. I found it helpful to know God was with me in my situation. My favourite being "My words do not return void but accomplish what I sent them out to do." I firmly believe God hears our prayers and that when we pray for healing, although we may not see the physical manifestation, God is at work on the inside.

This truth being confirmed during a time of receiving prayer for the healing of a whiplash injury which was further aggravated by a car crash in which I was sandwiched between two cars. Amazingly, no one got hurt and after waiting for the police, we gave up and drove home. While they were praying for me, I saw *the insides of me*; it was quite strange. I saw something move and wondered what it was. Holy Spirit flashed a memory into my mind, of many years before.

I was asked to teach on a particular Sunday morning after our senior leader said he was not up to preaching. None of the elders wanted to do it. They turned to me and said, "You do it." Throughout the previous night, and for the whole week prior, God had been instructing me on unforgiveness. This was a first for me: I had spoken at our *Ladies'* meetings but never preached to the whole congregation. I agreed to speak as if this was perfectly normal for me. It was a supernaturally inspired message on forgiveness; I stood and delivered what the Holy Spirit was saying, totally relying on him with no backdrop of notes to rely on, and full of *His* confidence; which was so unlike me. Halfway through the message, my confidence nearly wobbled when an angry-looking man stormed out rather noisily, slamming the door and distracting myself and the audience. I wondered what I had said to offend him but soon got back into my stride. The Holy Spirit, as they were praying for me afterwards, whispered forgive him.

To paint a clearer picture, some churches did not believe that women should teach or preach in those days. Some viewed it as heresy. Also, the sudden request to preach had not given me any time to consider that it was a first, for our church. The word was well received, with many acknowledging their need to *forgive* while many responded to the altar call and forgiveness.

The angry man disappeared from our church, returning many years later, and I had completely forgotten the instance. But now the memory was replaying as if it were present. I watched with fascination as the angels got a hold of this *thing* in my body and removed it as I forgave. The pain was still there in my neck but slightly reduced and as I testified to this later, I sensed a lightness in myself.

The Healing coordinator at my churches' Healing Centre asked me and my colleague to pray for this same man. What a coincidence this was, having not seen him for quite a while and with what the Holy Spirit had now shown me. I wondered if he would want me to pray for him. I voiced my thoughts to him, knowing there were other teams available to pray for him. To my surprise, he knew instantly what I was referring to and said, "I have always meant to ask your forgiveness for being so rude and arrogant."

I was then curious at what had offended him, and he said my message was riveting which was why he stayed so long, but a woman speaking and God using her to bring conviction, was too much for him as he did not believe women should preach or teach. Both our hearts were right towards each other and God healed him.

Marvelling afterwards, at God's love and how He orchestrated it all, He knew ahead of time I would one day pray for the man and wanted no hindrances to his healing or mine. He had come in a wheelchair and shortly afterwards, could walk without the excruciating pain of which the doctors could find no cause.

This absolutely convinced me that when we pray as Isaiah 55:11 says, "So shall my word be that goes forth from My mouth; it will not return to Me empty, without accomplishing what I desire, and without succeeding in the matter for which I sent it." We may not see the manifestation as we expect to see it, but God is at work and he knows what we need best. Maybe a good prayer would be; *Holy Spirit, show me what you are up to, so we can partner with you.*

Learn to Forgive. I meet many people who have felt let down, disappointed by leaders and betrayed. When they have recognised the betrayal and forgiven those concerned, healing sometimes comes to all areas of their lives: physical, emotional and spiritual. Maybe you have felt hoodwinked, betrayed or deceived by a leader. We believe the lie that our leaders are perfect - they are not; they are just like you and me and we all have bad days.

For many years I allowed myself to be emotionally and spiritually abused by a leader; making excuses for him and believing the lie he fed me: I was at fault. One minute he was praising me, the next, tearing me apart. In those days, we were taught not to question leaders. Incorrectly using the scripture: 'Do not touch Gods anointed.' I have known churches that tell their people not to stay friends with people who leave their church. How hurtful this is! *So, when a person leaves the church are they to lose most of their friendship groups too?*

A few weeks after recognising the betrayal of a church leader and choosing to forgive, one person encouraged me when she acknowledged, "You don't know what a difference that prayer has made to my life; I can trust again; a heavy load of guilt has disappeared."

I have experienced massive disappointments not just with Alistair, but in other areas of my personal life, work, friendships, and ministry. As I mentioned earlier, we have a choice either to let them make you or break you. Looking back, it has moulded me more in those hard times than in any other time. God once showed me a picture, I was a cracked clay vase with holes and bumps, then I saw him put his hands lovingly on this clay vase smooth out all the cracks and bumps and became under his hands a beautiful vessel which he then brightly painted and put on display for all to see.

I had to accept people will disappoint me, life can disappoint, it is part of life, but God promises he has good plans for us, plans to prosper and not to harm us, plans to give you a hope and a future. Last, keep pressing close to God and know these feelings will pass. You have a daddy with arms outstretched, ready to hug and comfort you. Run into his arms and tell him how you are feeling: frightened, insecure, wanting to cower away. He already knows how you feel and not shocked by what you want to say. He will come and feed you and rescue you, but he waits for you to let him.

Angels

Chapter 10

THE POWER OF THANKFULNESS

When Alistair was about six years old and attending Grange Park School, (a local school for children with special needs) I still had to dash here, there and everywhere keeping up with his appointments. During this period, Richard picked up a bottle of my perfume and before I could grab the bottle, he had sprayed it into his eyes. This resulted in a dash to the accident and emergency department where they discovered he had a squint, causing him to be slightly cross-eyed. We were reassured that an operation on his eyes would correct this and the best place for this to happen, was at Great Ormond Street Hospital.

I ended up juggling appointments, for both boys, which was no easy task. When it was time for Richard's eye operation Alistair was also in hospital for a week to evaluate his drugs and progress. At first, the appointments worked out really well but trying to split me between the boys, was very difficult. I was determined to be with Richard before and after the operation, but Alistair's doctors now also wanted to meet with me.

God made a way, as Richard's operation time was changed, and I managed to speak to Alistair's doctor team before rushing to the other end of the hospital in time for Richard to be given his pre-operation drugs. Whilst he was in the operating theatre, I rushed back again, helped feed Alistair to be back in time for Richard waking up from the operation. It turned out that Richards' eyes were much worse than they had thought. I then wondered what would have happened if he had not squirted the perfume into his eyes. The consultant mentioned, if they had not rectified it, the problems with his vision might have caused him problems in later life. The operation had taken much longer than anticipated but was a complete success. Richard needed to wear a patch over his eye for a while. At first, he did not like it but when we all called him Captain Richard the Pirate, he kept it on.

PRISON TO PRAISE

Fortunately for me, during this stressful period, whilst at the hospital, I came across a small book titled Prison to Praise by Merlin Carothers which I read and reread quickly, as I could not believe what it was asking me to do! *"To be joyful always, pray continually, giving thanks in all circumstances for this is God's will for you."* Thessalonians 5:16-18. (NIV) "What? How can I praise God about Alistair? And praise God for Daniel's death? You must be joking! With Richard now facing an eye operation!" But the book emphasized how the Prayer of Praise is the highest form of communion with God and is one which always releases a great deal of power into our lives. Praising Him, it explained, should not be something we do because we feel good; it is an act of obedience. Often, the power of praise happens with sheer teeth-gritting willpower. Yet when we persist, somehow the power of God gets released into us and into the situation. At first, in a trickle perhaps, but later, in a growing stream that finally floods us and washes away the old hurts and scars. Merlin goes on to describes how God painted a picture on the screen of his inner vision.

"I saw a beautiful, bright summer day. The air filled with light, and I had a sense of everything being exquisite. Up above was a heavy, solid black cloud beyond which I could see nothing. A ladder extended from the ground up into the black cloud. At the base of the ladder, were hundreds of people trying to get a chance at climbing the ladder. They had heard that above the blackness was something more beautiful than a human eye had ever seen; something that brought unbelievable joy to those who reached it. As person after person tried to ascend, they quickly climbed to the lower edge of the clouds and the crowd watched to see, what would happen.

In a short, while the person would come wildly sliding down the ladder and fall into the crowd scattering people in all directions. They reported that once they got into the blackness; they lost all sense of direction.

My time finally came, and as I made my way up the ladder into the blackness, it grew so intense that I could feel its power nearly forcing me to give up and slide back. But step by step I continued upward until suddenly my eyes beheld the most intense brightness I had ever seen. It was a brilliant whiteness too glorious to describe in words. As I came out above the dark cloud, I realised I could walk on top. As I looked into the brightness, I could walk without difficulty. When I looked down to examine the nature of the cloud, I immediately sank. Only by looking at the brightness could I stay on top. Then, the scene changed, and I was back looking at all three levels from a distance. "What does it all mean?" I asked, and the answer came:

"The brightest sunshine below the cloud is the light that many Christians live in and accept as normal. The ladder is the ladder of Praising Me. Many try to climb and learn to praise Me in all things. At first, they are very eager, but when they get into things they don't understand they become confused and cannot hold on. They lose faith and go sliding back. As they fall, they injure other people who have been hoping to find a way to live in continual joy and praise.

Those who make it through those difficult times reach a new world and realise the life they once thought of as normal, cannot be compared to the life I have prepared for those who praise Me and believe I carefully watch over them. He who reaches the light of the heavenly kingdom can walk on top of difficulties no matter how dark they may seem. As long as he keeps his eyes off the problem and on My victory in Christ. No matter how difficult it may seem to trust Me, allow me to work in every detail of your life. Keep clinging to the ladder of praise and move upwards!" The above extract is used with permission from the author's organisation and the book can be bought at http://www.foundationofpraise.org.

During this time, I kept praising God that he would work it all out, and although HE DID putting this truth into action was at times tough for me. Yet I became determined to climb up the ladder of praise, thanking God for all the things in my life. Gratitude to God welled up in my spirit and when tormenting thoughts flooded my mind, I sensed I was falling back down the ladder. I chose to hold on, gritting my teeth. Anytime the tormenting returned, I would turn them around and exalt God for knowing the beginning to the end. I reminded myself that his word says he will turn everything around for good. Even when I didn't see it, I chose to believe God, rather than my circumstances as I knew he was working behind the scenes and so I praised him for his goodness.

While feeding Alistair one day, I set this act into motion. He was taking longer than usual to get through his food. Normally, it would take an hour and a half to feed him and I found myself losing patience, but I chose to praise God saying, "I will praise you that Alistair is taking ages to feed, I will enjoy this time with him." As I did this he started to co-operate, and before long we had finished. I noticed a change; from then on, I enjoyed feeding Alistair, no matter how long it took. I learnt to appreciate the time with him. I shared with others about the ladder of praise and how we are to be joyful always, praying continuously and giving thanks in all things.

People around me put this praise mind set into practice too and we all individually saw changes in our lives. Not only was I happier, but it seemed to affect all those around me.

One time, I shared this at our fellowship's ladies' group and afterwards received an excited phone call from one of them. After the meeting, they were travelling back home in a car full of the ladies, when their car broke down on a deserted road. None of them knew what to do so they laid hands on the bonnet and commanded the car to work, then thanked and praised God while wondering, what He would do. "Maybe, He would send an angel, or someone would stop to help." She recalled. They looked around; the road was still deserted with no sign of an angel. So they carried on praising Him, enjoying their extra time together. She carried on, "Then one of them said, 'We have prayed. Let us try to start the engine again.' We continued to pray and praise as she inserted the key into the ignition, the engine started immediately, and we all made it home safely." Her husband insisted she took it to the local mechanic who found nothing wrong and waived the bill.

I loved this testimony and the one below thy both helped shift my way of thinking, accepting and viewing life. No matter how difficult it may seem to trust God to work in every detail of our life, we must keep clinging to the ladder of praise and move upwards.

BIRD IN A DESERT

Another analogy was of a bird that lived in a desert. It was sick, with no feathers, nothing to neither eat nor drink and no nest for shelter. One day, a dove was passing by, so the sick, unhappy bird stopped the dove and inquired, "Where are you going?" The dove replied, "I am going to heaven."

The sick bird said, "Please find out for me when my suffering will end?"

The dove said, "Sure, I will," and bid goodbye to the sick bird. When the dove got to heaven, it shared the message of the sick bird with the angel in charge at the entrance gate. The angel said, "For the next seven years of its life, the bird will continue to suffer, with no happiness till then."

The dove said, "When the sick bird hears this, he will get disheartened. Could you suggest a solution for this?"

The Angel replied, "Tell him to recite this verse: Thank you, God, for everything."

The dove on meeting the sick bird again delivered the message of the angel to it.

After seven days, the dove was passing by and saw the bird was happy. Feathers had grown back on his body and a small plant grew in the desert area. A small pond of water was also there, and the bird was singing and dancing cheerfully.

The dove was astonished because the Angel had said there would be no happiness for the bird, for the next seven years. With this question in mind, the dove went to visit the angel at heaven's gate. When the dove put forth his query, the Angel replied, "Yes, it is true there was no happiness for the bird for seven years but because the bird kept reciting, 'THANK YOU GOD FOR EVERYTHING,' in every situation, his life changed."

CAST ALL YOUR CARES UPON ME

It is so easy after a while, to forget what you have learnt. Alistair was going through a particularly frustrating time and we were having disturbed nights. I should say 'I' was having disturbed nights as my husband and I agreed, I would do the night times as he had to leave for work at 5 pm. It was the school holidays and Alistair, now nine years old, was out of his routine and missing the stimulation at school. I was tired, fed up and finding it hard to pray and thank God. Then the Holy Spirit said to me, "Cast all your cares upon me, my yoke is easy, my burdens are light." I started to give him all my cares. Then he said, "What about the rest?" I continued pouring out my heart about the sleepless nights, how hard it was to find the energy to cope with Alistair and Richard during the day: lifting of Alistair, changing him, trying to keep him and Richard occupied. Alistair also had a sore on his leg from wearing legsprints, which the doctor was keeping an eye on plus, an ever-streaming nose from a cold. Richard needed my time as well and so did my husband. We were both exhausted by all this. Then in my mind's eye, I saw the Holy Spirit take off this yoke from me, put it in a wheelbarrow and wheel it into a fire. Then Jesus emerged from the fire carrying my yoke upon him. The Holy Spirit again repeated "My yoke is easy; my burdens are light." I felt so much better after this and started to thank him again.

PRAYER

As mentioned previously, I knew little about prayer apart from how Jesus taught the disciples to pray *The Lord's Prayer*. I learnt how to pray during the few hours leftover from when Alistair would not sleep and needed comforting. He would wake up screaming in pain and no matter what I did, it practically did not work. Prayer, however, was the only thing that *worked*. I would pray for God to heal all disabled children. Then I would pray for their parents or caregivers, as Holy Spirit directed. Many years later, during an operation on his legs, we found out that he had a twisted muscle in his knee; this explained why he used to wake up screaming. The amazing answer to this prayer never caused him pain during the day.

What is prayer? I found out that as I partnered with God, the Holy Spirit would reveal Heaven's plan for me and others, on earth. I saw this as a partnership between me and God - declaring the will of God on earth. I would pour out my heart and in two-way communication; he would reveal his heart and purposes. Prayer, I discovered gives God the legal right to act on our behalf. As I reasoned with God, I would sometimes find that my will and desires were contrary to God's: often leading me to repentance and brokenness.

Apart from praying during my free few hours, I had no discipline to pray. *The Joy of Prayer*, written by Larry Lea helped me with this. Jesus made a habit of prayer, and he taught others to pray by his words and example: "*Can you not tarry one hour with me?*" In the gospels, we discover the most exciting work Jesus did was to pray. Overflowing with anointing and compassion, He went from a place of intercession to receive the fruits of the battles he had won in prayer: mighty miracles, authoritative revelations, wonderful healing and powerful deliverance.

I would pray: "Father God, I want Jesus' anointing put a desire within me to pray more: to grow in love with praying just as Jesus did." One benefit of Alistair's appointments was that they gave me time to read books as we waited our turn to see the doctor. Little did I understand that the Holy Spirit was awakening my heart to pray; revealing new and hidden things about prayer that I had not known before - shaping my future and destiny.

As I meditated on the words, 'Our Father' He became *my Father* and as I let my mind dwell on Him I pictured him as the Father I had always desired. A father who protected and listened; who celebrated me as a person without conditions: loving and available. Forgiving me without reminding me of my fault and, not critical. I became excited as the truth sunk into my heart that this was the character of my Father God - a Father who loved me unconditionally.

Maybe as you read this, you are having problems with relating to Father God as your Father. I too had problems, and I needed to forgive my earthly father for not being there for me; for being an absent father, often working until late: always being tired and exhausted by the time he returned home. Until then, my picture and beliefs about my *heavenly father* were that he too *did not have time for me*. You can ask Father God what lie or lies you have believed about him. Ask where that belief came from. This might come as a memory, a picture, a sense or feeling. Press into it, confess and forgive were necessary. Then ask for truth or what he wants to give you in exchange for those lies.

I prayed:

Father God; you are my Abba Father, all these years I have compared you to my earthly father, forgive me for believing the lie that you are too busy to spend time with me and not available when I need you. I praise and thank you for being my, Abba Father and thank you for allowing your son to die on the cross for me. Help me replace the lies with truth and enable me to break every habit in my thought life.

I discovered, by making declarations I was affirming my faith whenever I turned my thoughts into declarations of faith and praise. It says in Psalm 100:4: *We are to enter His gates with thanksgiving and his courts with praise.*

I also came to understand the Lord 's Prayer is an outline, and the word hallowed means 'to sanctify or set apart; to praise; to adore'. It expresses an intense desire for God's name be recognised: set apart and adored. The name Jehovah, or 'I AM WHO I AM' could be interpreted as 'I am with you, ready to save and to act, just as I have always been.' I started studying God's names. I already knew a few, Jehovah-Jireh my provider from Don Moen's song known by the same name.

I started discovering so many different aspects of Gods names:

Jehovah-Tsidkenu - the Lord My Righteousness: God made him who had no sin, to be sin for us. He makes us clean. This means I can pray to Him. Jehovah-Tsidkenu thank you for forgiving me my sins and making me clean. Your word says, "If we confess our sins, he is faithful and just and will forgive us our sins and purify us from all unrighteousness. I praise you that you are our righteousness." (1 John:9).

Jehovah-shalom - the Lord my peace. Jesus made peace by the blood of his cross and brought reconciliation. His peace which passes all understanding let it guard my heart and my mind. You are the peace in every storm. By honouring God's name, I remember who he is and what he has done for me.

Jehovah-Rohi the Lord my healer, the word Rohi means to restore, cure or heal, not only in the physical but also in the spiritual and moral sense. And I pray on that aspect of his name until I get the release to move on - praying for each member of my family and others to be healed, body, soul and spirit. Then I ask for the anointing of healing to be normal in my church. Thinking of people who need healing, praying and thanking God that by his stripes they are healed (see Isaiah 53:5).

When I get stuck in prayer, I bring out the list of all the meanings of his name.

Your kingdom come; Your will be done, on earth as it is in heaven. (Mathew 6:33) NIV. But seek first his kingdom and his righteousness, and all these things will be given to you as well.

A light-bulb moment came when many things were impeding with putting God first in my life. Priorities seemed to be my church, husband, my children, then God, when I had time. Determined more than ever, to put God first. Quality time with God was now top on my list, rather than when I had spare time. Interestingly, as I did this, the other things which had got in the way, slotted into their rightful place and life became less stressful.

I became mindful of so many members of my family in need of Jesus as their saviour and those in the world. I prayed for people to cross my paths, so I could share with them the good news and for God to remove any veils on their hearts and make scales drop from their eyes. I prayed that the eyes of their understanding be enlightened and open to the truth of the gospel.

The harvest is plentiful, but the workers are few. The Bible says, "Ask for the Lord to send out workers into his harvest field. I noticed the need for growth in my evangelism but also the call for others to do the same. I prayed that we would trust and have confidence in the Lord; that we would be like trees planted by the water, sending out roots by the stream, never fearing and bearing much fruit. I asked for strong roots that could not be uprooted; for a people of faith, full of His wisdom, being transformed into the image of Christ; bringing about his will on this earth.

Come into my life, in my marriage, in my children, in my workplace, in my business, in my ministry, in my church. I invited him to assume his place in my heart and to rule my spirit, soul and body; to build me up in power and might, that Christ may dwell in my heart through faith. I prayed that I will be rooted and established in love and that I may have the power, together with all Gods people to grasp how wide, long, high and deep is the love of Christ, and to know this love that surpasses knowledge filled to the measure of all the fullness of God. (Ephesians 3:17:19. Then I continue to pray in tongues knowing this is the perfect prayer for me and others.

I discovered as I prayed for my leaders, that I had a responsibility to petition, pray, intercede and give thanks not only for them but also for kings and all those in authority.

"I urge then first of all, that petitions, prayers, intercession and thanksgiving be made for all people
for kings and all those in authority that we may live peaceful and quiet lives in all godliness and holiness. This is good and pleases God our Saviour, who wants all people to be saved and to come to the knowledge of the truth." 1 Timothy 2 1:4 NIV

The scope of people to pray for became wider and the aim of the prayer clearer. Again, I was reminded of the power of thanksgiving with the request that our lives be spent in peace and tranquillity so that all men might be saved and come to the knowledge of the truth. As I prayed, it reminded me that Father God desired that none should perish but for all to have eternal life. Prayer is putting love into action.

Give us this day our daily bread

The word 'daily' jumped out and I pondered on what *daily* meant for me. My conclusion is that 'this day' is talking about the present. Instructing me not to worry nor get anxious about today or the future as Father God will supply all that I needed: each day. It is also a promise of on-going provision.

Daily bread includes not only my physical needs but my spiritual, relationships and emotional needs. God cares for the entirety of my whole being. The verse reminded me of Israel's Exodus, on their way from slavery to the Promised Land; fed with bread from heaven. As bread, often symbolises the word of God, I realised Jesus was not only meeting their physical and emotional needs but spiritual needs too.

My prayer became: *Thank you for promising to provide for all our daily needs, physically, emotionally, relationally and spiritually. Father God, daily you know my needs and that of my loved ones. Help me not to think and worry about the future and may there be leftovers to help others.*

Jesus points out in the next verse, there is a condition to his promise.

..and forgive us our debts as we forgive our debtors

Jesus died for me and took upon himself all my sins and transgressions. When I asked him into my life, he wiped all my sins: past, present and to come. I was reminded of his word, *"If we confess our sins he is faithful and just to forgive us our sins, and to cleanse us from all unrighteousness."* 1 John 1:9. NIV.

Therefore, if I'm forgiven, I have no excuse to hold resentment, bitterness grudges, unforgiveness or anger towards myself or others. I remember hearing someone say, "Let your debtors go, allow God to be the judge." I thank God that my parents modelled forgiveness to each other. They instructed us to always say sorry to each other and makeup. This I tried to model in my life, marriage, in fact with all my relationships.

I remember one time praying and asking God's help for my relationship with our eldest son as we seemed to end up arguing and shouting at each other. I was taken aback when the Holy Spirit said, "Ask for his forgiveness." He was standing on our grass bank looking forlorn. As I uttered those simple words, "Please forgive me," tears fell down his face as he said, "That means a lot to me." He hugged me and said he was sorry too after which the shouting stopped.

Sometimes we don't realise the power of forgiveness. I once was counselling a young lady who hobbled in wincing, then carefully sat down. She shared about past abuses and ended by saying angrily, "I will never forgive him even though I know the bible says I should."

"It sounds like you need help with being able to forgive," I said.

"Yes," she admitted.

"What about we ask Jesus to help you?"

Before we prayed she saw a vision of Jesus looking at her with much love. She described how shame and repulsion lifted off her, as she reached for his hand. Jesus then gently changed her heart towards her abuser, by showing her how the man was also repeatedly abused in his life. She forgave her abuser, repented of her hatred for men, and the anger she had towards them. As she did, she felt the tight ball of anger within her stomach and her anxiety, disappear.

What a miracle of healing, unfolding before me!

Not only was she healed from her hurt but also physically. The pain went, and she walked out, not needing a stick.

...and lead us not into temptation but deliver us from evil.

When I first read this, I thought, "How I need delivering from the temptation of chocolates!" One was not enough; before long I would have scoffed the whole box. This passage teaches us not only about prayer but about daily living as a Christian. The Lord's prayer divides into two sections, the first teaches us things we need to know about Father God and the second teaches us those things we are to know about ourselves.

The problem is not the temptation of chocolates but the greed that came as the result of eating a few. I was reminded, Jesus also faced temptation but was without sin. He has given us an escape route.

"No temptation has overtaken you except what is common to mankind. And God is faithful; he will not let you be tempted beyond what you can bear. But when you are tempted, he will also provide a way out, so you can endure it." 1 Corinthians 10:13.

God is faithful: not allowing any temptation (that is too great for us to resist) come our way. He will always provide a way for us to say no and the strength to bear up under the pull of sin.

"We do not want you to be uninformed, brothers and sisters, about the troubles we experienced in the province of Asia. We were under great pressure, far beyond our ability to endure, so that we despaired of life itself. Indeed, we felt we had received the sentence of death. But this happened that we might not rely on ourselves but on God, who raises the dead." 2 Corinthians 1:8-9, NIV

The above verse seems to cancel out 1 Corinthians 10: 13, but God is not saying we will not have to endure trials, tribulations hardships, temptations. His word promises, *"He will never leave us* or forsake us. We are to rely on God and not be self-sufficient asking for his help when we need it.

Psalm 121 1:2

I lift up my eyes to the mountains — where does my help come from? My help comes from the Lord, the Maker of heaven and earth.

...but deliver us from evil.

Ephesians 6: 10 says, *"Finally, be strong in the Lord and in his mighty power. Put on the full armour of God, so that you can take your stand against the devil's schemes. For our struggle is not against flesh and blood, but against the rulers, against the authorities, against the powers of this dark world and against the spiritual forces of evil in the heavenly realms."*

We know that the devil prowls around like a roaring lion, but we can pray, deliver us from evil and do our part not to allow any openings of sin or by our language cancelling out our prayers.

To summarise the Lord's Prayer is an outline and there are many ways of putting it into action.

God loves Worship and when we worship Him, there is power in his name. By declaring his names, it reminds us how powerful and great is our God.

Thy kingdom come thy will be done

Father let your kingdom come in my life, my family, my marriage; I give you my will. Let my will, be your will and change me to conform to your word and ways. Transform me into your image with ever-increasing glory.

For yours is the Kingdom and the power and Glory.

It is His Kingdom and all power honour and glory belong to him. Nothing is too hard for him.

We have an enemy who is trying to steal from us and destroy us. But we pray from a place of victory empowered by the Holy Spirit. Ask God to show you any lies of the enemy you believe and as you repent ask him to show you the truth. Remember He promises to supply all our needs, physically, emotionally, relationally and spiritually.

CHAPTER 11

GOD MAKES OUR PATHS SMOOTH

One night, I had a dream, and in it, the Holy Spirit gave me instructions to listen to what my husband would say, as He would be guiding him. I awoke puzzled by the dream. As we were having breakfast, my husband said, "I have been thinking about this work you are doing down the church, and I believe you need professional training as a counsellor and the church should pay for it." Remembering the dream, I replied, "Sounds like a great idea but they have never paid for anyone's training before." I was amazed when the senior elder said they would pay for my training, as it would benefit the church. They paid for me to do an Introduction to Christian Counselling course and paid for me to attend other courses I asked for.

Over time, the need for inner healing and deliverance became less, and other churches were now having their own teams. This freedom allowed me to concentrate more on the counselling side. I was appointed the church's counsellor and whatever was above my level of expertise, I referred elsewhere. All the above happened after an impartation at a ladies' day.

WHEN DESTINY CALLS

During those early years of being a Christian, myself and some women from my church used to attend a residential ladies' conference at High Leigh: hosted by Eileen Vincent and her daughter Rachal Hickson. One of these conferences radically changed my life. Eileen Vincent prayed for me, and for the second time in my life, I was slain in the spirit. I was so overcome by the power of the Holy Spirit's presence; I fell on the floor.

"Whilst out in the spirit,

> I see Jesus standing by my feet, looking satisfied with what is happening and watching as I feel bolts of electricity going through me; lifting my body off the ground. Looking at Jesus, I wonder what is going on. I hear Jesus in my spirit say, "You will never be the same. I am preparing you for your destiny." When I get up after being on the floor for over two hours, I make my way back to my room rather shakily.

Even though it was now the evening, the encounter had felt like minutes, not hours. I shut my eyes to go to sleep and immediately saw a *vision. I was holding a sword cutting through thorns and thicket, surrounded by ancient doors. But it was not just cutting the thicket. It appeared to be clearing the way. The sword was cutting the roots away, then the thicket fell, and the ancient doors opened. I heard rejoicing and singing as the light of the Lord shone through the darkness. The demons fled, and Jesus walked right in and the captives walked free.* Isaiah 49 came to mind.

The next day, as I sat reading my bible, I had another *vision. The room changed into techno colour before my eyes. There were lots of fires, all different sizes. I saw myself experiencing great difficulty in igniting* some fires. Some were being blown frantically and looked as if they were about to go out. Then I watched as sparks flew out, starting other fires. Some of these developed into enormous blazing fires which people could not put out, and I knew I would be part of this. I heard the Holy Spirit say, "You will make ways for people and make their paths straight. I will use you to light fires and other fires you will blow on, by the wind of my spirit. Some you will pour fuel on, and they will become a blazing fire. Many fires will spread in nations."

Back from the conference, our church asked us to share testimonies (stories) of our encounters that weekend. These testimonies, and the change in us, totally changed our church so much so that men became envious of what we had encountered.

Suddenly, I had such a heart for our women. I prayed for them crying out to the Lord, night and day, "Give me a Women's ministry." My prayer was soon answered, and it happened much quicker than I had imagined. We had often talked amongst ourselves and asked why we had no ladies' conferences ourselves. We decided we would have our own in-house ladies' day conference. The women, much to my amazement, asked me to lead it. I agreed, but others would have to do all the administration and organising since I had less spare time.

The programme comprised four people sharing their testimonies, and I was asked to be the main speaker. Up until the day before the conference, I had no direction on what to speak about, and hardly any time to seek the Lord. Then a friend gave me a list about what, *Focusing on Self,* rather than God could lead too.

Recently, I found the notes I had prepared for that conference (based on that list) and wondered how I was able to preach God's word for a whole hour. People said they enjoyed the testimonies and the word. The day was declared an outstanding success. Ladies from other churches heard about it and wanted to come to the next one.

The following year went back to Heartcry Women's Conference at High Leigh. Only this time, I had an agenda to collect names of women who were interested in attending a more local women's conference.

God, however, had another agenda. Eileen Vincent picked on me while ministering. She suddenly stopped talking and pointed at me saying, "I call you to the Nations, I have appointed you as a leader, and you will do mighty exploits for me." Mentioning healing and restoring, she carried on prophesying for over ten minutes and to be honest, a lot of it went over my head, as I was sure she had chosen the wrong person. I stood there thinking, "Is she talking about me?" When she finished, she touched me, and I went flying over two rows of people, taking out chairs, hitting people, and landing with a thud that jarred me. No one came to any harm. I examined myself for bruises later, and I was amazed, there were none.

Many years later, my friends said they thought she was prophesying to the wrong person, and they, like me, thought the word was probably for someone behind me. I wonder if that was why God propelled me over the rows of chairs.

After the conference, I returned with an assurance of the authority in Christ bestowed on me. The elders recognised this change and appointed me the leader of the prayer ministry teams. Then a while later, they confirmed me as leader of the women. Over sixty women in the church expressed their excitement and asked when the next ladies' day would be.

In 1997, we advertised our first ladies' day conference open to others, and I was delighted that Rachel Hickson agreed to be our speaker. We advertised through letters to all the people who had given me their addresses and told them to tell their friends to come. Over a hundred women attended and their overall feedback was that in their own churches, they had little opportunity to receive prayer and to be ministered to. Also, they often were responsible for the children. At our conference, they felt free to ask for prayer and felt like they had been ministered to.

I remember not knowing how to pay Rachel and gave her all the offering, coins and all. The look on her face alerted me that this was not the normal way. I had no idea that normally, people were paid by writing out a cheque to them.

They say anointing is 'catching'. As I ministered alongside Rachel, my anointing grew as I received words of knowledge on how to pray. People got healed physically and emotionally, judging by the number of tears.

The Ladies' Days grew in popularity, with leaders from London churches attending with their women groups, as well as more women from the local churches also registering to attend. The speakers were selected by the leading of the Holy Spirit. He would drop a name into my mind for the next Ladies Day and I would think, "Who the heck is that?" Shortly afterwards, someone would mention the very name and it would turn out they knew them personally. I remember Liz Doyle well; she spoke about evangelism in a way which removed the fear so much so, the ladies could not wait to practise evangelism. The elders granted permission, as long as I led it.

I had never done door-knocking before, neither had any of the women. We met beforehand at the church, prayed and then went out, feeling strongly led, to a difficult estate in Chatham. Liz had given us step-by-step instructions, which we carried out religiously. We knocked on doors giving leaflets about the church and offering to pray for any needs, and to those interested, we shared the gospel. It was quite an art keeping an eye on the teams, as people were disappearing into houses (to talk and pray with people) without alerting one another. That was our first time of evangelising. Thankfully, we pulled it off with no mishap, and new people attended church the following Sunday.

One week, we went out evangelising and discovered that people on one side of a certain street were welcoming but when we crossed over, the atmosphere was completely different. People shouted abusive remarks at us as we knocked on their doors. We prophesied around the estate and declared there would be a church planted there one day. This happened about three years later.

Once, a lady started to cry at her doorstep and asked us in - by now we had set up a system of letting others know if we entered a home. She was very pregnant, and I asked if I could bless the baby, to which she said the baby resulted from rape down a dark alleyway. I was surprised at her sharing this, as she had told no one else. I asked if she wanted to report it. She clutched at her stomach, horrified at the suggestion, as she felt it would have bad repercussions upon her. I offered to go to the police station with her, but she did not want to report it. We carried on sharing the love of Jesus and I blessed the baby in her womb, telling her how much God loved them both. I left my number in case she wanted to talk more, but she never contacted me.

Evangelism became a regular event. We prayed one week; the following week evangelised - praying as we walked around the estate. We researched the history of the area and prayed into what the Holy Spirit showed us. I later found out this practice is called spiritual mapping.

After two weeks, some felt brave enough to approach people on the street. The first time I did this, I felt tremendous intimidation and weakness at the knees, thinking loads of 'what if's'. I nearly chickened-out but others were watching me, so I finally screwed up the courage to do it. We choose a small group of boys who liked the idea of us practising on them. We chatted with them for a while and they told us they were Muslims. They allowed us to pray for them. The more we evangelised, our confidence grew.

The Ladies' Days were now so popular; we hosted an evening event for women leaders. Two visiting American prophets were our speakers: Mary Jean Pidgeon and Barbara Arbo. They gave us an understanding of how men think, as opposed to women and also dealt with *'shame issues'*. They encouraged women to come to the fullness of everything God had for them, not viewing themselves as second-class citizens. They spoke on Revival and Desiring more of the Holy Spirit. Nearly everyone responded to the altar call: even people who rarely respond. The Holy Spirit's presence was strong, and many went away with a prophetic word. One lady said at the end, "She would never be the same." God honoured us on the day, as we had called it *'Flowing in the Supernatural U.K. Women's Revival'*.

During this time, many opportunities opened for me and I found myself invited to attend different Women Leaders events. One time, looking out at the audience while sharing a stage at Westminster Hall with renown women-leaders - women I looked up to - I felt so privileged to be there.

I had an extraordinary experience at one of these leaders' meeting. The speaker was Jean Darnell. I arrived late, hot and flustered as I kept getting lost. She said, "Someone's spirit has just witnessed to what I have said about ministering to the broken-hearted and poor in spirit." My spirit had leapt at what she said, taking me by surprise. I did not know my spirit could leap and 'it' seemed excited.

She said, "Put your hand up if that is you". I put my hand up, expecting others to join me. She then asked all the other ladies to gather around me. There must have been over a hundred women-leaders who all took it in turns to pray and prophesy over me. I staggered out of there.

REFINED BY FIRE

The Ladies' Day event ended abruptly when our senior leader left. A new pastor was appointed, and he seemed keen for us to carry on with the deliverance and inner-healing ministry but recommended putting-on-hold the Ladies' Days.

Under the previous pastor's leadership, I received an invitation to speak at a Women's Aglow meeting, which I accepted. By the time it came to the meeting date, we had a new pastor in place. At the time, I was juggling church and family life - looking after Alistair, who was *on an intravenous drip,* in hospital. Keeping the drip on was a nightmare, as he kept pulling it out and being violently sick. A consultant said he believed Alistair was anorexic, which I laughed at, as he loved his food. The frustration I experienced with them not believing me left me feeling helpless. Alistair took matters into his own hands. The next night the staff became so tired of replacing the needles he pulled that they decided to leave his drip until morning. His vomiting stopped, and they realised he was allergic to the drip.

In the meantime, I suddenly realised I was due to speak that evening, at the Women's Aglow meeting. Thinking there was no time to prepare and panicking about what was I going to speak on, the Holy Spirit flashed scripture into my mind and said, "Speak about your life and what I have done." The night I ministered; I am glad I was unaware that their regional South East of England

Manager was in attendance. She came up to me afterwards and said, "I would like you to be an itinerant minister for us." She explained this would mean travelling to different Women's Aglow meetings and ministering to those attending. "I will contact you and tell you more," she said.

I had carried on counselling, by partnering with another Christian counselling centre who offered me free training. However, it soon became clear I needed a more consistent and advanced training than what I was getting as so many people were presenting us with complex, abuse issues.

Our new pastor suddenly informed me, that he was standing-me-down for over a month and from all leadership roles as he wanted to clarify to people that I worked for him and not our previous leader. He invited my teams to dinner at the Crest Hotel and even though I was aware of his intentions, it still hurt when he announced that he was standing-me-down for a month - with a question mark over what route would be taken, on counselling and deliverance. He however mentioned, he would still want me to pray for people during the meetings.

This was a very difficult time for me and the enemy encroached, whispering lies: I had done everything wrong. *It* pointed out all my mistakes - from a few things wrong to everything in my mind. Convincing me I was a lousy counsellor and the worst leader; no wonder he had stood-me-down! This state of mind continued for about two weeks; finding myself unable to pray, I felt wretched and adrift.

A member of my previous team phoned and said, "Whilst praying for you, God had shown me a vision of a raging bull charging at you, extremely angry. I feel God is saying you are to stand up to the bull, and He will give you the strength and boldness to do it."

Her words snapped me out of my hopelessness and I came to my senses, recognising the accusations as lies. Instead of coming against the lies, I needed to come against the Father of Lies, the devil who was the accuser. Instantly, as I repented, I felt this enormous weight of oppression leave me. Then I got angry at the devil, the instigator of the lies. I decided to use the time to pray, seek God and read his word and turn the situation around.

After a month, I received a phone call from my pastor asking me back. At a meeting, he outlined his plans for me which sounded exciting. His wife would naturally take over the leadership of the women and he wanted me to carry on counselling and to become a volunteer in the office. My husband agreed, but my petrol money had to be paid for and I would only work until 4 pm, to be home in time for Richard's return from Art College.

I enjoyed working for the new pastor and I seemed to have a good working relationship with him. However, when I spoke to him about becoming an itinerant minister for Women's Aglow, he went berserk and questioned why they had not asked his wife instead. I was refused permission to take on the role and the pastor threatened to throw me out of the church if I pursued the call as Women Aglow also expected me to set up a local group.

Months later, I approached him (the pastor) about further training, as a counsellor. This time, he was much more amenable, and we came up with a plan to open the training up to others who were interested in Christian counselling. I had done my previous training with Barnabus Training Consortium, so I felt they would be a good place to start.

When I rang them, they were excited, as they had just been praying about finding an opening for training in the South East of England. They agreed to run a course at our church for two years and offered me a free place if I agreed to be the administrator of the course. There were twenty of us on the course: meeting on Friday nights and all day, on Saturdays.

Unfortunately, the pastor changed his mind about using the newly trained counsellors just after we all qualified as advanced pastoral counsellors. He allowed me to remain in charge of the intercession prayer team and praying for people who had accepted Jesus, but someone else was coming in to do the counselling.

"God, what are you doing?" I asked. After hearing nothing, I repeated the question, this time changing it to "God, what do you want of me?" I heard, "I have many servants but few friends. I want you as my friend." Then he showed me a picture of me preaching to a crowd of people.

During this quiet season, I used the time normally spent counselling people to reading the Word, praying and finding out what scriptures say about being a *friend of God*. I learnt that friends of God obey his commandments and what is important to God, should be important to me too. I enjoyed the time to study and pray, now with time to see different people. It made me take stock of my priorities. I had been so tied up with volunteering at the church that I had neglected my friends and time with God as his friend. I had just been thinking about getting a part-time job, (with Richard not home until after 4 pm and Alistair at boarding school, only home for the weekends) when I received a phone call requesting me to see our pastor. This meeting resulted in me being reinstated as the church counsellor, and he also appointed me the departmental head of prayer. Intercession, ministry and salvation teams were now my responsibility. He wanted me to work for him, full time.

The sum I was paid was not the going rate, but it was more than petrol money and I enjoyed working at the church. I was counselling less, as people were now encouraged to see the new counsellor - one of our new elders who was studying for his counselling degree.

I was asked to help set up the new Caring Hands project for the Homeless. So, I helped one of our leaders with the administration and set-up needed, but this did not last long as he expected me to work five days a week, taking away my only free day, Monday – which was given as compensation for working on a Sunday. He could not understand my resistance to this and no matter how hard I tried to explain that I needed a day off to do my housework, he did not see the need for this.

OLD SKILLS MEET NEW SKILLS

I gave in my notice but before I could leave, I was offered another job as Grant Manager by our Senior Pastor. This meant applying for grants on behalf of the church. The fact I had no experience in this field did not seem to matter to him. He said I would learn on the job. Which I did. It was a steep learning curve as I also had to come up with viable projects that would benefit the church, and then apply for funding. This training came-in useful years later, when we needed to set up projects.

I was successful at three bids, but it was a soul-wrenching job. For every application sent in (which could take weeks, even months of work) the success rate was one in five or one in ten, some months. Someone with more experience came along and I was offered a new job to coordinate the church events and projects we won bids for. Prior to this period, we held very few events. When I said *yes* to coordinating church events, I did not envisage our pastor was thinking big.

Our first event was a Bandstand Barbecue Open-air event in June 1998 and was held for the community, attracting 4,000 to 5,000 people. While organising it, I had a dream and saw a marquee tent with a board outside saying, *'Do you need prayer for depression, anxiety, anger, divorce, marriage problems, children etc.?'* During the planning meeting with leaders from other local churches, I shared this dream, and they decided we could have a prayer tent - a first for the UK!

Each church took a certain aspect of the day. Our church was in charge of the BBQs and supplying the manpower needed for this. A different church took on the role of stewards, and another security. It was my responsibility to organise the attractions and to coordinate the overall event: reporting to the senior pastor and company secretary.

My previous training of organising Alistair's exercise team and Ladies' Days now helped with running these bigger events. The overall responsibility of coordinating over 300 volunteers and their supervisors, plus liaising with their appropriate church leaders, was scary and proved quite a challenge. There were six other churches involved, but my fears proved unfounded as God gave me help when I needed it. I took the scripture "Cast all your cares upon him," literally and formed the habit of giving the problems to God before I went to sleep, and in most cases awoke with a solution.

A big challenge was erecting security-fencing right around the perimeter of the event. One of our members - a builder, was helpful in telling me how many panels to order. He also helped supervise the erection of panels. I was unaware that God was downloading all the skills I would one day need as I went along.

The weekend before the first event, the whole church turned out and we cleared Victoria Gardens of any rubbish, debris and broken glass. The council were so impressed that they bent over backwards to help us. They even installed new electrics in the bandstand. The first year, we had the army help us, after a meeting with the Colonel in Chief, persuading him to erect army tents and provide an assault course. This was the first experience I had of having my car checked for bombs.

I thought I was superhuman and agreed to manage the prayer tent and the event, not understanding what could go wrong on the day. Did the first event run smoothly? No. I was rushing around all day.

I had no idea of all the problems that could happen on the day of an event. We had miscalculated by 1,000, the number of buns needed for the day and I had to persuade Tesco to ask their baking team to bake another 1,000. We also needed 1,000 more beef burgers; I emptied their freezers out. Plus, I needed to negotiate the purchase at a fantastic price. We offered Tesco's free publicity, and I got the burgers at an incredible price (but understandably) they were not willing to deliver them.

We also had not factored-in the overuse of the church toilets, but bless them, the ladies of the church stepped in, cleaned and stocked them without even letting me know about the problem until afterwards.

The next year, we went bigger and had marquees, but making the mistake of not having security officials assigned to guard them. Fortunately, I had included insurance in our quote as the chandeliers were stolen. The police recovered everything shortly afterwards. They told us some youngsters had crawled under the flaps of the marquees. We quickly learnt to have no valuables near those flaps. Another church stepped in, to provide night time security. They were having such a good time of fellowship and worship; they had no problems getting volunteers to stay the night. The offer of a cooked breakfast also helped as an enticement. The police offered to police the event. What a bonus!

Before we opened the event to the public, we would always pray. As we prayed for our third Grandstand Barbecue, peals of thunder and lightning were happening all around us. To our dismay, the heavens opened the ground awash with water, putting out the BBQ fires. We are watching the rain in horror when a young man got up on a chair and commanded the rain to stop. As quickly as it started, the thunder and lightning ceased. The chairs we wiped down but even those dried in a few minutes with the heat of the sun. The ground was completely dried up, with no sign of rain. The sun blazed for the rest of the day without a cloud in the sky.

The church had sent me on a course on how to write newspaper articles and media requests. My expertise in this field worked for me as Radio Kent turned up and did their Road show from the gardens. They advertised our event over the air by encouraging people to come and watch them. The previous year, we had difficulty keeping up with the demand for sausages and burgers. This time, much to my relief, there was no shortage of food, having calculated the catering needs correctly. The barbecue teams were exhausted by the end of the event. The newspaper reported 5,000 to 6,000 attended. They loved the fly wall, bouncing castle and face painting which was all free. We also ran a competition to find the best singer.

The stage was erected on a Swain lorry. Looking back, I took for granted the favour we had. My senior pastor's event experience whilst working for Reinhard Bonkee was invaluable. He taught me how to make the trailer look amazing with skirtings and backdrops. In the evening, we did a youth event with a well-known Christian group: resulting in over a hundred people, asking Jesus to be their Lord and Saviour.

Each year, the bandstand barbecues became bigger. One year, we got a Jet flyover to raise money for Kent Air Ambulance but on the day, they had not organised people to man the collection-tins. Promptly, I was able to roundup trustworthy people, to handle the money donated towards the show. Liaising by mobile phone with the pilot, was a challenge in a noisy open field. The roar of his jet engine drowned me out. At one time, because of the clouds, it seemed the jet flyover might have to be aborted but suddenly it appeared, to the roar of the crowd. The air show which had taken months of preparation was over in seconds, but it had been well worth it, as we raised a healthy amount of money for the Kent Air Ambulance.

The following year, we published a newspaper called *The Son*, and I was sent to persuade our local Mc Donald's Manager to accept them and pay for advertising in it. I met with the Area Manager, who offered us the clown Ronald McDonald as a guest at the next bandstand barbecue. This, at once, brought us media-attention, and parents brought their children to see Ronald McDonald.

One year, before the portable toilets could be collected the next day, someone tried to steal them at night. In the process of removing them, they started to roll down a grass bank, spilling its contents everywhere but the smell must have put them off. Much to the senior pastor's annoyance, he was called out by the Police in the middle of the night, to arrange for Medway Environmental Department to clean up the area. His fury was still apparent when the next morning he gave instructions that I walk around the site to check no tent pegs or rubbish had been left behind (normally, we would both do this or with others) then I was to stay back until the portable toilets had been collected. I wondered what the hiring company would say but apparently, they were used to worse cases and it was no problem to them. Toilets they said, had been recovered from car parks and peoples' gardens in the past.

In 2000, we started holding Bible Weeks at the Central Hall Theatre, with seating for one thousand people. Compared to the barbecues, these events had different challenges as I had to liaise with well-known speakers, checking their needs were fully met. *Cannon and Ball, Tommy Tenny, Dick Eastman, John Bevere, Paul Scanlon, Andy Elmes, Tom Griffiths,* Sue Renaldi, *The World-Wide Message Tribe and Vinesong* were just some of the ministering guest

I attended to. One year, I remember rushing around to hotels, with baskets of fruit which I had forgotten, to deliver, earlier.

Mostly, the pastor did the liaison with the speakers and he also arranged the transport. My part was to coordinate with all the various teams. I remember the sound technician being most impressed at the questions I asked him - not knowing this is my husband's field of work. I had to work out all angles and check they were well covered. Our prior experience of recruiting volunteers to steward and handle the security needed for these weeks was invaluable.

One time, I had to collect a renowned, music band from Uganda at Gatwick Airport. Unfortunately, in my panic about driving to Gatwick, I forgot to ask which terminal and what their names were. When I eventually arrived there (after getting lost) no one would answer the phone in the office to give me the information needed. In desperation, I asked the airport officials to announce over the Tannoy (then a popular brand-name for loudspeakers) for a group from Uganda, 'playing at a church on Sunday' to please make themselves known to Ann Hubbard, who was waiting for them at the information desk. To my relief, it worked, but no one had told me they were expecting a van to pick them up with all their equipment and suitcases.

I coordinated these Bible weeks for many years, meeting well-known speakers. John Revere stood out for me, as I had suggested him as a speaker and the fact he agreed to come, marvelled me. He was so humble and unassuming, not providing a long list of needs. The Holy Spirit gave him a prophecy for our church, which the leadership was not happy about. Part of it said, "God would spit us out of his mouth unless we repented." The Senior Pastor had looked at the number of people being saved and not at our lives. So, he ignored it. The after-party was uncomfortable, but John Bevere took it in his stride.

A year later, the Senior Pastor was asked to leave. I wonder now, whether things would have been different if the Senior Pastor had taken that prophesy seriously, and we had all (as a church) repented. Instead, there was a very messy *parting of ways*. We went from being a very prosperous church with no debts to one with massive debts which, to the new leadership team's credit, was repaid over the years. This episode rocked many and people fell away from God.

The previous day, to the showdown, another leader came to tell me *what had been going on*. I was shocked at the revelations and wondered how I could have been so blind. The next day I came into work as normal, I was one, out of twenty staff, and we had all lost our jobs. As we stood outside in shock, one after another, people said the same thing: "*I feel free, it's like a hold over us, has been broken.*" I suddenly became more aware of the fog-like veil but had not recognised at the time, that we had come under the influence of a Jezebel spirit. My friend walked up to the driveway and asked what was going on. She advised: "You can use this to make you or break you." Consciously, I decided this would *make,* and not break me.

Some members of the church staff struggled to forgive, but I knew it was vital to keep my heart right. I was determined to guard myself and let no negative words against this leader came out of my mouth. The Holy Spirit worked on my heart and showed me I had a great deal to thank him for. He showed me that even though this pastors actions towards me bordered on abusive, he had believed in my abilities, set me tough challenges and consequently, I had become a skilful organiser and administrator.

I had believed in a lie (before working for this pastor) that I was not intelligent, but stupid. The Pastor would constantly say' "You are highly intelligent" and then show me examples of this. He would remind me of when I had walked into a leaders' meeting and was called upon resolve an impasse with another leader. I was there just to bring refreshments in, as the meeting was taking longer than normal. The senior leader turned to me, explained the problems and said, "Have you any ideas?" It seemed clear to me, so I made suggestions. They looked at me in astonishment and all agreed my input was a brilliant idea and that it should work.

One day, something shifted, as I began to believe what the pastor had said. It dawned on me that all my life, I had compared myself to my brothers and sisters who all had university degrees. I had allowed verbal and emotional abuse from this pastor until the day I woke up and faced the reality of what was happening. From then onwards and on behalf of myself and the staff, I became an advocate for the bullying to stop. The Holy Spirit said, "One day, you will be a leader of hundreds, and I want you to learn from this, *what not to do."*

The Bible says, "All things work together for good for those who love the Lord…" and I have witnessed this in my life again and again. The day after being made redundant, I was flattered when I was contacted and offered a job as Executive Personal Assistant to the owner of a Christian TV company, and also appointed the channels Intercessor. It was my dream job. I prayed about it but did not get clear direction on whether to take it or not.

I soon learnt that all that glitters, is certainly not gold and so I left the job, being owed over £3,000 as the boss would repeatedly say, *'I cannot afford to pay your salary this month. Would you mind a partial payment and I will make it up the following month?'* One month, he would pay me fully, but not making up the partial (outstanding) payments, as promised. At an event, some God Channel executives warned me against him, but I ignored the warning.

By this time, I had changed churches and my new pastor asked me to work for him. He wanted me to design an access database and help him start a scheme for Freshers. I discovered this meant new university students. God opened a wide door with Greenwich University, Medway campus and they welcomed us with open arms as they were still reeling from the suicide of an overseas student who had not come out of her room since arriving.

I met many international students. Some were scared at first by the number of new people they encountered. Also, many were freezing cold, often not having any coats or jumpers. I took many a student on shopping trips to buy jackets at Primark. We would pick them up on a Sunday, provide fellowship and a hot dinner. Some had no hot meals during the week. We did this for a few months until other members of the congregation also invited them back, home for lunch.

The students' accommodation varied. One of them was provided with no heating until we purchased a heater for him. When I visited the home of another student, I was shocked by the appalling state of his room and stunned that any landlord could rent out accommodation with such poor living conditions. The student was content and said it was better than where he had lived, back in his homeland.

Six months later, I became the phone-line coordinator for a charity in Maidstone. This was a new post and when I read the job specifications, it was like someone had written the requirements with me in mind. One of the specifications was some experience of running a phone-line and organising volunteers. Now this experience and that of running events opened the way to them giving me the job.

After the Bible conferences, one of the television companies bought our videos and televised them at 12 pm. They also asked us to run a contact prayer-line and to be available after the broadcast. In my role as head of the prayer team, this was my responsibility, so I also ended up volunteering myself. I believe this experience was one of the keys to them offering me the job. It was an interesting time. Some nights, I received a few phones calls. Some of these calls were abusive, and other nights, we would be kept busy, praying for people. We received many encouraging messages of gratitude for praying with them. This role became bigger and bigger and by the time I left; I had the role of project coordinator. I handled coordinating eight-hundred clients, two-hundred and fifty volunteer-befrienders and running the daily phone-line with ten volunteers. It was fun arranging days out which usually involved a good lunch, pantomimes, shows in London, shopping twice a week, exercise classes and other activities. Having access to two minibuses helped make my life much easier.

When my boss slipped on ice and broke his hip, as a matter of urgency I had to take over running the project. The next day, we were holding a Christmas party for more than a hundred older people. This was whilst undertaking an introductory degree in counselling, run by Greenwich University. Talk about juggling many balls and different hats!

Studying at Greenwich University in 2008, and for the next three years, was simply out of God's favour. I had a clear word from the Holy Spirit telling me he wanted me to train as a secular counsellor and then pointed to where the training should be. At every church meeting, there would be a word about God changing my direction. I went back to the Holy Spirit, reminding him I did not have adequate qualifications to get into a university.

He seemed to ignore my doubts, and I filled in the application form in obedience. I was surprised when asked to attend for an interview and test. The test was an essay on a traumatic event in your life on two sides of an A4 sheet of paper. All I could remember about writing essays was beginning, middle and end. It must have been okay, as I had an interview the same day.

They said my impressive experience as a Christian counsellor counted as the qualifications needed and I was offered a place with the condition that I attended their summer school on how to research and write essays - which I had not done in over thirty years.

The counselling training requirement meant I had to have placements at different agencies and have personal counselling myself. I was already working four days a week. Where was I going to fit this in? I asked myself, but God was so good. When God asks you to do something he will make a way where there seems to be no way. I did my personal counselling of 150 hours during my lunch hour within the building at my workplace and the placement hours were also within the building. After my daily job, I would walk downstairs, putting on my counselling hat.

The aim of our project Brighter Futures was to aid elderly people of sixty-five years and over to maintain their independence and reduce admissions to A&E and nursing homes. This meant they were able to stay in their own homes for as long as is practical. I had the chance to share the gospel with many of them during day trips and whilst assessing new clients' needs. Many of them ended up asking Jesus to be Lord of their lives, and others recommitting their lives. This project was so successful; we ended up winning a lottery award and the Queens Award for volunteers. This led to my husband, I and some volunteers being invited to the Queen's garden party at Buckingham Palace. Another item ticked off my dream list. We also did an event for the Lord Lieutenant of Kent and Kent County Council, which also won us an award - God does honour those who honour him.

Sometimes, God asks us to do things we would prefer not to, like being available on the phone line from 12 pm to 1 am and later: on busy nights. Yet this did not enthral me, though God must have known the skills I had learnt would be required for the next level of my destiny. All my years of running events, overseeing the volunteers and ministering through prayer, God knew that the experience I had gained would make handling the expansion of the older person's project an easy task.

I did not understand God's plan, purpose and destiny for me but when Father God said, "I am sending you to the nations" all those years ago, whilst with him in heaven, I had no clue I would stand in front of over 1,000 people and preach in Zimbabwe, Zambia and the United Kingdom; representing Esthers for the Nations.

Now I shudder when remembering the fear and intimidation I used to experience before I spoke - it was immense! If I could get out of sharing or giving a word, *I would*. Until, I learnt to do so, while still being afraid. I soon realised that as I stood to speak, the fear would lift. I could never understand why I had so much fear since I loved

God: until I attended the second year of the European School of Supernatural Ministry held by my church. During a lesson, the teacher instructed us, to ask the Holy Spirit to show us anything stopping us from believing we are creative.

The Holy Spirit flashed into my mind's eye a picture of me standing in a corner, wearing a dunces' hat. Then it flashed back to when I was reading out loud: stumbling over my words. What happened next, I had not remembered, but the children were encouraged to laugh at me as I stood there, in shame. From that day on, I had hated school with a passion and gave up trying to excel. After the humiliation, *I was sent to Coventry.*

Then the teacher said to ask the Holy Spirit, what it is that the enemy has stolen from us. The Holy Spirit said, "I have called you to be an orator of the word." From that day, all fear and intimidation left, as I forgave them.

At the last conference in Zambia, I had the privilege of speaking about spiritual warfare over a whole day, teaching out of some examples from my life. I enjoyed it tremendously and the day flew by with the Holy Spirit filling me with the right words to say.

Esthers for the Nations started in 2008. Florence Sutherland, our founder and President, was prompted by the Holy Spirit to raise women to pray and come into all that God has destined them to be by empowering, strengthening them through bible study, conferences and healing. The Holy Spirit prompting her to read the book of Esther and said she was called for such a time as this. Our organisation aims to empower women to pray and be all that God has called them to be. We have a support network of women who are there to support each other on a personal level. We support individuals through donations, gifts, bible study and prayer. Our aim is to have prayer groups in every village, town and city both in the UK and abroad. We also bring our professional skills to the ministry to help and support others. We have counsellors, coaches, social workers, doctors and nurses on our team. This extensive bank of Resource helps us meet people's needs effectively.

EFN has a presence in many countries, including Pakistan, Zambia, Zimbabwe, New Zealand, Kenya, Ghana and the United Kingdom. We are listening and open to going wherever the Lord would have us go. We also hold conferences to share knowledge, encourage and build each other up. We partnered with other organisations to help educate orphans and fund different projects. Our annual conferences are well attended; the same applies to our smaller healing conferences, held throughout the year. This year will hold our tenth annual conference.

When God's word advises not to despise small beginnings, I had no idea what He was referring too. The road to getting here has not been easy but in hindsight, the difficult times have been some of the most precious, memorable learning times.

God Makes our Paths Smooth

CHAPTER 12

END FOR NOW

End for now

Recently, Annie Kelly a Christian physiotherapist and craniologist massaged and manipulated different parts of my anatomy. My body soon started releasing traumatic memories stored within; often referred to as *somatic memories*. My brain kept receiving flashbacks from Daniel's birth to other traumatic memories as if I was reliving them.

I was suddenly back in time, listening to Dr Mathews, Alistair's consultant from Great Ormond Street reading the autopsy report of Daniel's death. My body shuddered as I reheard him say he had an incomplete stomach and a twisted leg. I remembered feeling like such a failure as a mum, at the time.

Then the Holy Spirit reminded me of when at seven years old, Richard was diagnosed with dyslexia. This also fed into my inferiority complex, making me believe I couldn't have healthy children. Most of my life I had felt inferior. (I wipe away the tears as I write this). I remember Rachael Hickson saying, *"You are a giant-of-woman in the spiritual realm even though you see yourself as a grasshopper. One day you will outstrip me, but you need to get rid of your grasshopper mentality."* She prayed for me to be blessed with a triple anointing and I received it but until this day, I had always held myself back; not realising why.

The Holy Spirit spoke, through my sobs, *"You are not imperfect; you are perfect. I made you perfect. It is just 'circumstances that happened' I have been with you every step of the way, I am in front of you; I am behind you; I am around you."* I started to sob, at the realisation of His kindness and love towards me. God was there first. The memories flashed by and my stomach got warm. I felt a sensation of release as if the stored trauma in my body moved down to my feet. Annie coincidentally started to work on my feet and I felt completely relaxed as the trauma left my body.

The belief of being a failure had been reinforced at school with my scores being mostly, third to last in examinations; crowned by the constant name-calling and bullying. This sense of failure was all again, reinforced when baby Daniel died.

When Alistair was in a frog-leg plaster (his legs were separated by a wooden broom handle) I was upstairs and being prompted something was wrong, entered Alistair's room to find, he had suffered a *grand mal* epileptic fit. The force of the fit had turned him over and he was unable to get his head out of the pillow which was now covered in vomit. He suffocated and suffered asphyxia.

I had blamed myself for further brain damage. I remember at the time being worried they might think I had done *it* deliberately. I had also been haunted by thinking the nurses and doctors were watching me. When I started getting paranoid with these thoughts, I managed to break the lie and accept; they were monitoring Alistair: not me.

End for now

As I typewrite this final chapter, I brush away my tears from memories flooding back. Now I am able to experience the emotions I couldn't process during the traumas. I hear the Holy Spirit say, "Forgive yourself." Even though I always believed I had.

So, Father God, I forgive myself for believing the lie that I was responsible for Alistair's further brain damage, and for all the other times I had believed I was to blame.

The physiotherapist left me with instructions - to rest in God's glory and to allow Him to carry on healing me. I was drenched in tears, from top to toe.

Dear God,

> *I have had so much loss in my life. Yet everywhere I go, you are with me. Every step of the way, you have been with me. Thank you for that, but it has been hard. It has been so hard. Even as I cry, I feel the Holy Spirit telling me that: I am ready for what he has ahead of me now. He will skyrocket me to eminence. I wonder what He means.*
>
> *Holy Spirit, I want what you want for me. Oh, Father please let this book bring life, deliverance and healing to others. Give them hope where they need it.*
>
> *Please let this book bring people closer to you; I want your name to be glorified. Let your goodness, love and kindness*

> *to shine out through it. The truth is **You are there for us all** just as you have been there for me. You said, "I have been with you every step of the way." Just as you said you would when Daniel died. You said I would be a mother to many and You will never leave me. Lord, you have never left me. Right now, I feel your presence. Oh wow! God, you are so good, you are so good; you are so good!*

The truth is, I had always compared myself to others and I would put myself down; I did not allow the negativity to stop me and would rise above it. But now I believe this day that Jesus has broken the power of the lies and I will struggle no more. I will be that person whom God has called and created me to be. I will walk out my destiny with my head held up high. No more will shame and humiliation come near me. I am not a failure; I am not inferior. I am a child of God, clothed (joyful at the truth) in royal garments; seated with him in heavenly places. He had shown me this, many times; I had felt it and known it in my head but deep in my heart, may be I had not accepted it. But today, I accepted it.

I am a royal daughter, princess of the King of Kings, the Lord of Lords and am seated in heavenly places with him. Wow, I carry his DNA and I will fulfil his prophetic words over my life.

Father God,

You are the accelerator! All the years when I have not truly walked in my destiny, are over. Now I run with arms open wide towards to my destiny; knowing you have equipped me. You are my enabler. You are the one who empowers me, and I have nothing to fear or to prove. I can just be me. Thank you, Lord, for this. I feel the Holy Spirit saying, "Today you are stepping into your destiny, and you are ready for it." I wonder what that means.

I pray that as I lay hands on people in your name, the blind eyes will see, the deaf will hear and the lame will walk. People will get out of their wheelchairs and walk; healed body, soul and spirit. Use me to help and bring healing to people with mental illness. Help me to reignite fires in your people and destroy the lies of the enemy. People will declare your Glory. Lord let my life bring great glory to you. Hundreds of thousands will come to know you. That's all I want Lord - to be a Glory Carrier in Jesus Mighty Name.

The End for now

Ann would love to hear from you with any feedback from this book and what you would like to hear about in a future book on spiritual warfare called "Keeping Safe"

You can also advance order a copy by contacting her at:

Email: - annhubbard2000@yahoo.co.uk

Printed in Poland
by Amazon Fulfillment
Poland Sp. z o.o., Wrocław